"Alvin Plantinga's magisterial *Warranted Christian Belief* is one of the most important works on the epistemology of religious belief within the last century. It is exciting to see the core ideas of that great work presented here in a more succinct and accessible format. *Knowledge and Christian Belief* is a pleasure to read and will serve as an excellent and engaging introduction to Plantinga's most influential ideas about the rationality of religious belief."

— MICHAEL REA
University of Notre Dame

"A very clear, easy-to-understand, and challenging presentation of the main steps of Plantinga's argument in his magnum opus *Warranted Christian Belief.* Using the tools of modern epistemology, Plantinga defends a classical position — that Christian belief does not need to be supported by any arguments from generally agreed premises in order to be fully rational, and that that belief cannot be shown to be false by any such arguments."

— RICHARD SWINBURNE
University of Oxford

Knowledge and Christian Belief

Alvin Plantinga

WILLIAM B. EERDMANS PUBLISHING COMPANY
GRAND RAPIDS, MICHIGAN

Wm. B. Eerdmans Publishing Co.
2140 Oak Industrial Drive NE, Grand Rapids, Michigan 49505
www.eerdmans.com

26 25 24 23 22 21   10 11 12 13 14 15

Library of Congress Cataloging-in-Publication Data

Plantinga, Alvin.
Knowledge and Christian belief / Alvin Plantinga.
pages   cm
ISBN 978-0-8028-7204-3 (pbk.: alk. paper)
1. Faith and reason — Christianity.   2. Apologetics.
3. Christianity — Philosophy.   I. Title.

BT50.P535   2015
230.01 — dc23

2014044388

Contents

Preface

My book *Warranted Christian Belief*[1] came out more than a dozen years ago. I still endorse nearly everything I wrote there; but some have told me the book is too long and in places too technical. I'm afraid I have to agree, and I would like to put things right. The result of my trying to put things right is the present book, *Knowledge and Christian Belief*. It is a shorter and (I hope) more user-friendly version of WCB. There are some changes of emphasis and a few changes of other sorts; but for the most part I follow the contours of WCB, adding a bit here and there, and of course subtracting a great deal of the detail. I've deleted the more difficult portions, but otherwise have used the words of WCB as much as possible. My hope is that the result will present the same ideas as the original, but in a briefer and more accessible fashion.

The chief topic to which the book is addressed is the question of the *rationality,* or *sensibleness,* or *justification,* of Christian belief. Of course this has been an important question for a good long time, going all the way back to the beginnings of Christianity, and becoming considerably more insistent since the eighteenth-century Enlightenment. This question has become even more important recently, with the so-called New Atheists bursting upon the scene. The central members of this outfit are the dreaded Four Horsemen — not the Four Horsemen of the Apocalypse, nor the legendary four horsemen of Notre Dame, but the four horsemen of Atheism: Richard Dawkins, Daniel Dennett, Sam Harris, and (the late) Christopher Hitchens. Their aim, it seems, is to run roughshod over religious belief.

Although the New Atheists are certainly inferior, philosophically

---

1. New York: Oxford University Press, 2000. Hereafter I'll refer to this work as WCB.

speaking, to the old atheists (e.g., Bertrand Russell, C. D. Broad, and J. L. Mackie), they do seem to make a good deal more noise. One might say they are more style than substance, except that there isn't much by way of style either; their preferred style seems to be less that of serious scholarly work than of pamphleteering and furious denunciation. They blame everything short of bad weather and tooth decay on religion. They conveniently ignore the fact that modern atheist ideologies — Nazism and Marxism, for example — were responsible, in the twentieth century alone, for far more suffering and death than religion in its entire history. Their style emphasizes venom, vitriol, vituperation, ridicule, insult, and "naked contempt";[2] what's missing, however, is cogent argument.

Nevertheless, some of their questions need answers. Among their claims is that religious belief in general and Christian belief in particular is irrational, can't sensibly be held, and must be rejected by anyone who is well educated and thinking straight. Thus Dawkins: "the irrationality of religion is a by-product of a particular built-in irrationality mechanism in the brain."[3] And according to Daniel Dennett, the "god faculty" is a "fiction-generating contraption."[4] With respect to the thought that *faith* is or can be a source of knowledge independent of reason, Dennett is not encouraging:

> if you think that this common but unspoken understanding about faith is anything better than socially useful obfuscation to avoid mutual embarrassment and loss of face, then either you have seen much more deeply into this issue that any philosopher has (for none has come up with a good defense for this) or you are kidding yourself.[5]

But how exactly are we to understand this complaint? In just what way is Christian belief irrational or intellectually disreputable? It's not easy seeing precisely what this claim of irrationality amounts to, and part of my aim is to get clearer about that. Once we've seen just what this claim is, I'll

---

2. See Richard Dawkins: "I am more interested in the fence-sitters who haven't really considered the question very long or very carefully. And I think that they are likely to be swayed by a display of naked contempt. Nobody likes to be laughed at. Nobody wants to be the butt of contempt." On Dawkins's blog, *RichardDawkins.net,* beneath a piece by Jerry Coyne, Wednesday, 22 April 2009 at 4:32 AM, #368197.

3. *The God Delusion* (London: Bantam, 2006), p. 184.

4. *Breaking the Spell: Religion as a Natural Phenomenon* (New York: Viking, 2006), p. 110.

5. *Darwin's Dangerous Idea* (New York: Simon & Schuster, 1995), p. 155.

go on to argue (1) that these criticisms, these claims that religious belief is irrational, are completely inconclusive; (2) that belief in God, and indeed belief in the whole panoply of the Christian faith, can be not only perfectly rational, sensible, and justified, but in fact a case of knowledge; and (3) that these objections to the rationality or sensibleness of Christian belief, if they are to have any cogency, must be based on the assumption that Christian belief is *false*. If am right, those who say something like "Well, I don't know whether Christian belief is true or false — who could know a thing like that? — but I do know that Christian belief is irrational, or unjustified, or not sensible, or not worthy of a thinking person" are mistaken.

A preliminary issue: some people seem to hold, oddly enough, that there really isn't any such thing as Christian belief and there really isn't any such thing as belief in God. The logical positivists, for example, claimed that sentences like "God loves us" or "God created the world" are vacuous and without content because they can't be "empirically verified." Others claim that our concepts don't apply to God, because he is so far above us, or because God is ultimate reality, and our concepts don't apply to ultimate reality. But if our concepts don't apply to God, then we don't have any beliefs about God.

So our initial question, addressed in Chapter One, is thus: Is there such a thing as belief in God? Is there such a thing as Christian belief? If not, of course, we needn't enter the question whether Christian belief is rational or reasonable. I'll begin by considering this Kantian-inspired thought, and will conclude, as you might have guessed (if only from the title of this book), that indeed there is such a thing as Christian belief.

Given that Christians do indeed believe the things it looks like they believe, I'll go on in Chapter Two to try to get a better fix on the claim that Christian belief is in some way sadly lacking — that it is irrational, or unjustified, or childish, or not worthy of contemporary people (people with our magnificent intellectual attainments), or in some other way intellectually lacking. What, exactly, is supposed to be the problem? There are several possibilities: one is that Christian belief is unjustified, where justification has to do with intellectual duty and obligation. This thought goes back to the classical foundationalism of René Descartes (1596-1650) and John Locke (1632-1704). I'll argue that it is easy to see that Christians aren't (or aren't necessarily) violating any intellectual duties in holding their beliefs. Another thought is that Christian belief, while it doesn't violate intellectual duties or obligations, is nonetheless irrational in some other recognizable sense. I'll argue that this is also untrue.

A third suggestion, owing to Sigmund Freud (1856-1939) and Karl Marx (1818-1883), is that Christian belief *isn't reality oriented:* the belief-producing processes or faculties that cause such belief aren't aimed at the production of true belief, but at the production of belief with some other property — perhaps the ability to carry on in the cold, cruel, heartless world (Freud) that we human beings find ourselves in. I'll argue that this is the most sensible construal of the objection we are considering. I'll also argue that this version of the objection is really the claim that Christian belief doesn't have *warrant,* the property or quantity that distinguishes knowledge from mere true belief.

In Chapter Three I'll look into the nature of warrant: just what is it? And why think Christian or theistic belief doesn't or can't have it? I'll give an account of warrant; then I'll show how theistic and Christian belief can indeed have warrant. I won't claim to have shown that such belief *does* have warrant (although I do believe that it does) but only that it *can* have warrant, and, if true, probably does have it. For if belief in God is in fact true (as I think it is), then very likely there is something like John Calvin's *sensus divinitatis* (or Thomas Aquinas's "natural but confused knowledge of God") by virtue of which belief in God, in the typical case, is indeed warranted. I won't argue that theistic belief *is* true, although of course I believe that it is. The fact is there are some very good arguments for theistic belief, arguments about as good as philosophical arguments get; nevertheless, these arguments are not strong enough to support the conviction with which serious believers in God do in fact accept theistic belief; furthermore, I don't believe that these arguments are sufficient to confer *knowledge* on one who accepts belief in God on their basis.

That's how things stand with belief in God; but I'll argue in Chapters Four, Five, and Six that something similar holds for full-blown Christian belief. For if Christian belief is true, then very likely there is something like Calvin's *internal witness of the Holy Spirit* or Aquinas's *inward instigation of the divine invitation,* and by virtue of these processes, Christian belief enjoys warrant. So if Christian belief is true, it is very likely warranted. Again, I won't argue that that belief in God or in "the great things of the gospel," as Jonathan Edwards calls them, do have warrant. That is because they have warrant only if they are *true;* and while I think they *are* true, I don't think it is possible to show, by way of arguments that commend themselves to everyone, that they are. (I do believe that there are strong arguments for their truth; but these arguments are not strong enough to confer knowledge on someone who accepts them by way of these arguments.)

Of course, even if Christian belief can be warranted, it can still be subject to objections and defeaters, reasons for rejecting or giving it up or for holding it less firmly. In Chapter Seven I will take up possible objections to theistic and Christian belief raised by J. L. Mackie, involving the relationship between warrant and religious experience. Then, in Chapters Eight, Nine, and Ten I'll consider possible or potential defeaters for Christian belief. Among these are, first, certain kinds of Scripture scholarship, the sort typified by, for example, the notorious Jesus Seminar. Biblical scholars of this sort very often come up with theories and conclusions incompatible with Christian belief; the question is whether their so doing furnishes a defeater for Christian belief. I argue in Chapter Eight that such scholarship, in its intention to be scientific, is constrained by *methodological naturalism;* I go on to argue that as a result the theories of these scholars don't (just as such, anyway) constitute a defeater for Christian belief.

Another proposed defeater is pluralism, the fact that there are many religions in addition to Christianity, and most of them are in conflict with Christian belief at one point or another. Suppose I recognize this: Does this recognition saddle me with a defeater for Christian belief? I argue in Chapter Nine that it does not (just as my recognizing that there are people with political or philosophical beliefs different from mine doesn't automatically give me a defeater for my political and philosophical beliefs).[6]

Finally, and perhaps most plausibly, there is the suggestion that the evil in the world, all the sin, and suffering, and pain, and anxiety gives a believer in God a good and perhaps conclusive reason to give up such belief. This is perhaps the strongest proposed defeater, and sin, suffering, and evil certainly do constitute a problem for many believers in God. Of course, this is nothing new; the Old Testament book of Job, for example, is a very early, very eloquent, and very powerful statement of this problem.

6. Still another proposed defeater that I do not take up in this book: various suggestions people make as to conflict between Christian belief and current science. Here there are several suggestions: that the occurrence of miracles, for example, the resurrection of Jesus Christ, is incompatible with science, that evolution is incompatible with Christian belief, and that the scientific mindset is incompatible with Christian belief. Still another suggestion is that current scientific accounts of religious belief give us a good reason to think such belief false or unwarranted. I have argued that none of these proposed defeaters has much going for it and that none of them does in fact constitute a defeater. Science and religion are, in my view, entirely compatible; the real conflict is between science and naturalism, the thought that there is no such person as God or anything like God. The interested reader is directed to my book *Where the Conflict Really Lies: Science, Religion, and Naturalism* (New York: Oxford University Press, 2011).

I argue in Chapter Ten that while evil constitutes a problem for believers, it is by no means a successful defeater.

For the most part what I say in this book follows what I say in WCB. There are a few differences. Some people complained that WCB seems irrelevant to Christians who have a less than maximal faith, Christians who suffer from doubts, uncertainties, etc. — as, of course, very many, perhaps most Christians do. I have tried to address this perfectly proper complaint on p. 67. This involves a fairly substantial change; apart from a few less substantial changes, what I say here matches what I say in WCB. I invite the reader who finds something incomplete or insubstantial about the treatment of a topic in this book to consult the fuller treatment in WCB.

Scripture quotations have been taken from the New International Version unless otherwise noted.

My thanks to Jim Bradley, Lee Hardy, Ann Plantinga Kapteyn, and Del Ratzsch, all of whom read the entire manuscript and made many useful suggestions. I'm especially in the debt of Lee and Del, who gave a whole new meaning to the expression "went over it with a fine-tooth comb."

CHAPTER ONE

Can We Speak and Think about God?

Our question in this volume has to do with the justification or rationality or reasonableness of holding Christian belief. But according to some, this is a non-question. That is because, according to these people, in reality there is *no such thing* as Christian belief. It's not that Christian belief is false, or foolish, or misguided; it's that *no one in fact holds Christian belief.* The thought is that it is *impossible* for anyone, any of us human beings, at any rate, to hold such belief.

Now this sounds pretty fanciful, to say the least: what about all those people who attend Christian churches every Sunday? Don't at least some of them hold Christian beliefs? Nevertheless this opinion — that there is really no such thing as Christian belief — is and has been surprisingly widespread. But why would anyone think a thing like that? Why think we can't have beliefs about God? Perhaps the most popular line of argument proceeds in the following way. Central to the Christian story, of course, is God, the all-powerful, all knowing, perfectly good creator of all. But according to this line of argument, we human beings can't have any beliefs about God; God is beyond all of our concepts; our minds are too limited to have any grasp at all of him and his being.

Kant

What reason is there to think that? The proposed answer is that God is *ultimate;* God is ultimate reality. But according to this way of thinking, we human beings are incapable of thinking about or holding beliefs about ultimate reality. Here those who think this way follow the great Prussian philosopher Immanuel Kant (1724-1804) in his monumental *Critique of Pure Reason.* As these people understand him, Kant teaches that there are really two worlds. On the one hand there is the world of *things in themselves,* things as they are apart from any intellectual activity on our part; on the other hand there is the world of *things for us.* The latter is the familiar world of experience, the world of houses and people and oceans and mountains. The former, however, is the world of things as they are apart from us, 'in themselves'; this world is entirely inaccessible to us.

Now Kant is by no means easy to understand, which is no doubt part of his charm. If you want to be a really great philosopher, make sure not to say too clearly what you have in mind (well, maybe that's not quite enough, but it's a good start); if people can just read and understand what you say, there will be no need for commentators on your work, no one will write PhD dissertations on your work to explain your meaning, and there won't be any controversies about what it was you really meant. Kant must have heeded the above advice, and the fact is there are dozens, maybe hundreds of books written about his philosophy, and endless controversy as to his meaning.

According to one historically popular interpretation, and the one relevant to our present concerns, what Kant was claiming is that it is we human beings, we ourselves, who confer its basic structure on the world — the world of appearance, the world we actually live in. For example, one very important structural feature of the world is that it consists in things that have properties. There are horses, houses, and howitzers: horses have such properties as being mammals, being able to run a mile in two minutes, being larger than the average dog, etc.; houses have such properties as being made of bricks, costing a lot, being good places to live, etc.; howitzers have their own rather military properties involving range, adjustability, etc. And according to Kant, at least under this popular interpretation, the fact that our world consists in things that have properties — that fact is due, somehow, to *us,* to our own intellectual or categorizing activity. It's a little like looking at the world through rose-colored glasses: the world looks that way, not because it really is rose-colored, but because of the glasses I'm wearing. Something similar applies here: the world as it is in itself doesn't have that thing-property structure, and in fact we have no way of knowing what sort of structure, if any, the world as it is in itself *does* have. We know the world only as it conforms to the categories of our mind, not as it is in itself.

According to Kant, therefore, there is the world of things in themselves, the world as it is in itself, and also the world of appearance, the world as it is for us. We are at home in the world of appearance, at least in part because we ourselves have constituted it, conferred on it, somehow, the basic structure it displays. But we have no grasp at all of the world of things in themselves. We can't think about these things; our concepts don't apply to them; they are in that regard wholly beyond us.

Now God, of course, would certainly be among the things in themselves. This strand of Kant's thought, therefore, would imply that we human beings can't think about God. We don't have any concepts that apply to God. Our concepts apply only to the world of appearance, not to the world of reality. Hence God, who is reality *in excelsis,* is so far above us, or beyond us, that our puny minds can't reach him at all. Our minds, and our thought, and our language simply have no purchase on God.[1] So some people who understand Kant this way, and think that Kant is fundamentally right about these things, conclude that we can't think about God. And of course if we can't think about God, we also can't talk about him.

Kaufman

Oddly enough, a fair number of theologians are very much taken by Kant, and think he is basically correct. They think that theology must just accept the main lines of Kant's teaching, and must be conducted under the assumption that Kant is fundamentally right. A good example would be the late Gordon Kaufman, for many years a professor of theology at Harvard Divinity School. In *God the Problem* he states the problem as follows:

> The central problem of theological discourse, not shared with any other "language game," is the meaning of the term "God." "God" raises special problems of meaning because it is a noun which by definition refers to a reality transcendent of, and thus not locatable, within, experience. . . . As the Creator or Source of all that is, God is not to be identified with any particular finite reality; as the proper object of ultimate loyalty or faith, God is to be distinguished from every proximate or penultimate value or being. But if absolutely nothing within our

1. I say this is one strand of Kant's thought, or perhaps one strand of Kant's thought interpreted a certain popular way; in other places Kant seems to say very different things, things that don't fit with this strand of his thought; again, that is part of his charm.

experience can be directly identified as that to which the term "God" properly refers, what meaning does or can the word have?[2]

The answer, given in his book *The Theological Imagination*, seems to be "not much," or at any rate "not much like what you would have thought":

> God symbolizes that in the ongoing evolutionary historical process which grounds our being as distinctively human and which draws (or drives) us on toward authentic human fulfillment (salvation).[3]

> "God" is the personifying symbol of that cosmic activity which has created our humanity and continues to press for its full realization.[4]

So our word "God" is not a name of an all-knowing, all-powerful, perfectly good Person; it is instead just a symbol of cosmic activity and historical process. Kaufman's problem with God (or "God") is that if God is in fact the creator of the universe and the ultimate reality, then he is beyond our experience; hence, following Kant, our concepts can't apply to him, and our word "God" can't refer to him; we have to think of some other function for that word.[5]

Of course this Kantian way of thinking can wreak considerable havoc with religious belief and with theology. One thinks of theology as telling us about God: what he is like and what he has done. One thinks the subject matter of theology is God himself. But if we can't think or talk about God, then nobody can tell us what God is like and what he has done. If we can't think or talk about God, then of course we can't think the thought that he has created the world, or is the Father of our Lord and Savior Jesus Christ, or hates sin, or whatever. If Kant (thus interpreted) is right, theology can't be about God; no one, not even theologians, can think about God, and if they can't think about God, they can't write about him. As the philosopher F. P. Ramsey once said, "What can't be said, can't be said; and it can't be whistled either."

Furthermore, when Christians recite the great creeds of the church

---

2. *God the Problem* (Cambridge: Harvard University Press, 1972), p. 7.

3. *The Theological Imagination: Constructing the Concept of God* (Philadelphia: Westminster Press, 1981), p. 41.

4. *Theological Imagination*, p. 50.

5. For a fuller account of Kaufman's thought, see WCB, pp. 32-42.

— the Apostles' Creed, for example — what they say can't really be true. They say, "I believe in God the Father almighty, creator of heaven and earth. . . ." But if our concepts don't apply to God, then we can't in fact believe that God is the creator of heaven and earth: for, of course, we could do that only if our concept *creator of heaven and earth* did in fact apply to God. Similarly, sermons in which the preacher preaches the gospel, the magnificent story of sin and redemption through the life and death and resurrection of Jesus Christ, the incarnate Son of God — these sermons too would be wholly misguided. The preacher would presumably be under the impression that she was in fact talking about God; but she would be absurdly mistaken. She literally wouldn't know what she was talking about. And of course the hearers would be in an equally absurd condition: they would be thinking that they were being spoken to about the great Christian story, when in fact nothing like that was occurring.

But why should we think any of this is true? Is there really a substantial reason for believing that we can't think or talk about God? The suggestion is that God is so exalted, so far above us, that we with our puny and limited minds can't hope to comprehend him. No doubt there is an appropriate caution here. And no doubt it is true that we can't comprehend him, if to comprehend God is to know a significant proportion of what there is to be known about God. But of course that doesn't mean that we can't think about God *at all,* and it doesn't mean that we can't know some extremely important things about God. Why should we think that we can't know or even believe the great things of the gospel?

Kant Again

As I say, those who think this way ordinarily are followers of Kant. Well, why did *Kant* think we can't talk or think about God? The suggestion was that it is because God would be among the "things in themselves"; and we aren't capable of thinking about the world of things in themselves, as opposed to the world of appearance. But why think *that?* The basic reason seems to be something like the following. First, there are some propositions we know without the benefit of *sense experience;* we can call this '*a priori* knowledge'. I know that nothing exists before it begins to exist; I don't have to go around investigating things to see if any of them exist before they begin to exist, finally concluding, after substantial inquiry, that none do. I know that all horses are animals; again, it would be absurd to

5

engage in some kind of survey, looking at a lot of horses to see what proportion of them are animals. ("Ah, here's a fine horse galloping around: now let's take a look to see whether it's an animal.") You know in advance that $7 + 5 = 12$ (this is Kant's own example); again, I don't learn this as a result of empirical investigation; I can simply see that it is true.

Kant thought, somehow, that we couldn't have this kind of knowledge, knowledge independent of sense experience, of the world of things in themselves. He found it puzzling in the extreme to see how we could have genuine knowledge that didn't depend on sense experience or empirical investigation. His proposed solution was to suggest that we have this kind of knowledge, all right, but only of a world we have ourselves somehow structured. We can know *a priori,* prior to experience, that $7 + 5 = 12$ because we have structured the world in such a way that $7 + 5 = 12$. It's as if we ourselves have put this into the world, and hence can know it. We are, so to speak, knowing our own handiwork.

But is Kant right? Why think that we can't have *a priori* knowledge of what is real? Couldn't God create persons who were capable of that? It's certainly hard to see why not. And might we not be creatures of just that sort? Again, it's hard to see why not. Further, couldn't God create creatures who were capable of knowing important truths about God himself? And might we not be just such creatures? Once more, it's hard to see why not. It's hard to see much of a reason, here, for this momentous suggestion that we can't so much as think about God at all.

Further, there is something self-defeating about this suggestion. If we can't think about God, then (as Ramsey said) we can't think about him; and therefore can't make statements about him, including statements to the effect that we can't think about him. The statement that we can't think about God — the statement that God is such that we can't think about him — is obviously a statement about God; if we can't think about God, then we can't say about him that we can't think about him. Perhaps there are things we can't think about, maybe things in some other part of the universe. If so, we can't pick out any of those things and say of it that we can't think about it.

Given the weakness of the argument (such as it is) for God's being beyond our conceptual grasp, being such that we can't think or talk about him, and given the fact that this view is self-defeating and undercuts itself, it seems the best course by far is to reject it. I shall therefore set it aside and proceed on the assumption that there really is such a thing as Christian belief.

CHAPTER TWO

What Is the Question?

Now many people concede that there is such a thing as Christian belief, but complain that there is something seriously wrong with it; Christian belief is irrational, or unjustified, or childish, or no more sensible than belief in Superman,[1] or in some other way cognitively not up to snuff, and therefore worthy of disdain and contempt. But what, more precisely, is the problem? Can we be a bit more specific?

De Facto vs. *De Jure* Objections

Beliefs can have at least two kinds of defect. On the one hand, a belief can be *false*. The *de facto* objection, with respect to a belief, is just that it is false, like the belief that there is such a person as Santa Claus. The *de facto* objector, therefore, argues that Christian belief is false, or at least very improbable. For example, there is the venerable "problem of evil": this is the claim that there is a contradiction between the facts of suffering and evil, on the one hand, and, on the other, the idea that there is such a person as God, who is omnipotent (all powerful), omniscient (all knowing), and perfectly good. God and evil are incompatible; but obviously there is evil; hence there is no such person as God. There are other versions of the *de facto* objection. For example, God is said to be an immaterial personal being — that is, a person without a body; but, so some followers of Wittgenstein think,

---

1. See Daniel Dennett in Daniel Dennett and Alvin Plantinga, *Science and Religion: Are They Compatible?* (New York: Oxford University Press, 2011), pp. 41ff.

it's not possible to be a person without a body.[2] Again, God is supposed to be both *omnipotent* and also *omniscient* but, so some people claim, it's not possible that there be a being who has both of these properties.

On the other hand, there is what I'll call the *de jure* objection, which also comes in several versions. Here the claim is not that a belief is false (although of course it might be); the claim, rather, is that it displays some *other* defect: it is immoral, or irrational, or foolish, or unjustified, or in some other way deficient. Consider the belief that there are an even number of stars; maybe that's true and maybe it's false, but it is not a belief a rational person will have (because it is the sort of belief for which evidence is required, and there is no evidence here either way). Similarly for the belief that the total snowfall at Mt. Rainier in the winter of AD 1895 was approximately 1205 inches. This belief is even less reasonable than the belief that the number of stars is uneven. With respect to what we know, it's as likely as not that the number of stars is even, but it is unlikely that the total snowfall at Mt. Rainier in 1895 was about 1205 inches: the highest total ever recorded there was about 1300 inches. Still another example: suppose I'm a baseball fan, and I firmly believe (perhaps by way of wishful thinking) that my team will win the World Series next year, even though they finished last this year and dealt away their best players. That too is irrational.

The *de jure* objection, therefore, is the claim that Christian belief is irrational or unjustified or perhaps immoral; more exactly, it is the person who embraces Christian belief who is alleged to be irrational or unjustified or in some other way deserving of disapprobation. This *de jure* claim is the chief focus of this book. It is also, I believe, far the more common of the two kinds of objections.

This objection is offered, first, by those who claim that Christian belief may have been sensible in the past, before the days of modern science, before we learned about evolution, relativity theory, quantum mechanics, and all the rest. But now, given contemporary science, it is no longer possible for a sensible and informed person to accept Christian belief. As I mentioned in the Preface (note 6), in the interests of brevity I'll simply refer the reader to my *Where the Conflict Really Lies: Science, Religion, and Naturalism*,[3] where I argue that while there is indeed conflict between science and *naturalism* (the view that there is no such person as God or anything like God), there is no conflict between science and religion.

2. See, e.g., Anthony Kenny, *The God of the Philosophers* (Oxford: Clarendon, 1979).
3. New York: Oxford University Press, 2011.

The *de jure* objection is offered, second, by those who emphasize the *pluralism* of religious belief. There are ever so many different and mutually inconsistent kinds of religious belief. There is Christianity, of course, but also Judaism, Islam, Hinduism, Buddhism, various African religions, Native American religions, and many others. Furthermore, some of these — Christianity, for example — split up into a multitude of warring factions. How, then, can it be sensible to embrace any particular one of these clamoring claimants? I'll respond to this objection in Chapter Nine.

Third, there are those who claim that it is *intellectually arrogant* to endorse a specific version of Christian belief, because then one is implicitly claiming that other people who *don't* endorse that version are inferior to you, or misled, or at any rate not as well placed as you are. Fourth, some claim that Christian and theistic belief, to be justified, requires *evidence* or *argument;* since there isn't sufficient evidence for it, so the objector goes on to say, such belief is unjustified. A fifth objection is that Christian or theistic belief is *irrational.* According to an important version of this objection such belief is a result of wish-fulfillment or wishful thinking. Thus according to Sigmund Freud (1856-1939), we puny human beings find ourselves in this cold, cruel world, and we can make life endurable only by projecting into the heavens a father who really does care for us (and is a lot more powerful than our human father). But such belief is irrational.

Now it looks as if any of these objections could be offered by someone who held no view as to whether Christian belief is *true.* The objector could put it like this: "Well, I don't know whether Christian belief is true or false; but I do know that a person can't rationally accept it (because there is insufficient evidence, or there are so many alternatives, or such belief is a product of wish-fulfillment, or . . .)." What I want to do in this chapter is to try to identify a *de jure* objection more exactly. What we're looking for is an objection (1) that really does apply to Christian belief, and isn't trivially easy to answer, and (2) is independent of the *de facto* objection — that is, is such that one can sensibly offer the objection without presupposing or assuming that Christian belief is false.

Is There a Serious *De Jure* Objection?

Let's start considering three of these candidates (those not dealt with in another book or a later chapter), beginning with

Christian Belief Is Arrogant

This is the claim that it is arrogant or egotistical to endorse or believe a proposition you know others do not believe. Thus William Cantwell Smith: "except at the cost of insensitivity or delinquency, it is morally not possible actually to go out into the world and say to devout, intelligent, fellow human beings: '. . . we believe that we know God and we are right; you believe that you know God and you are totally wrong.' "[4] Now strictly speaking, Smith seems to be talking about someone who doesn't merely believe what others don't, but who goes on to say out loud, so to speak, that what he thinks is right and what those others think is wrong. Gary Gutting goes a bit further; he argues that it is egotistical and arrogant to *believe* a proposition for which you don't have a good argument, and with which you know others disagree (whether or not you voice this belief):

> First, believing *p* [when I don't have an argument and know that others disagree] is arbitrary in the sense that there is no reason to think that my intuition (i.e., what seems obviously true to me) is more likely to be correct that that of those who disagree with me. Believing *p* because its truth is supported by *my* intuition is thus an *epistemological egoism* just as arbitrary and unjustifiable as ethical egoism is generally regarded to be.[5]

But is this really convincing? I believe it is dead wrong to lie about my colleagues in order to advance my career. I believe this very firmly. I know there are others who disagree: there are many people, people whom I respect, who doubt that there is *anything* that is really wrong (although some things may be inadvisable). I don't really have an argument for my belief here, or at any rate an argument that will convince those who disagree with me. But does it follow that I am arrogant or egotistical in holding this belief?

I don't think so. First, I don't really believe *p* on the grounds that it is supported by *my* intuition — that is, I don't reason as follows: *p* is supported by my intuition; therefore *p*. Instead, *p* just seems right. So suppose I think hard about this proposition that lying about my colleagues

---

4. *Religious Diversity* (New York: Harper & Row, 1976), p. 14.

5. *Religious Belief and Religious Skepticism* (Notre Dame: University of Notre Dame Press, 1982), p. 86.

to advance my career is wrong; and the more I think about it, the more clearly it seems to me that it's wrong. I consider all the objections I know: for example, reasons for thinking nothing, really, is right or wrong (although some things might be more advantageous or useful than others), or reasons for thinking that what counts, as far as right and wrong go, is only what is best for me and best advances my self-interest. After serious and protracted thought, it still seems to me, maybe even more strongly, that lying about my colleagues to advance my career is wrong. In fact it isn't even within my power, after thinking the matter over, to give up the belief that behavior of that sort is wrong. So could I be properly accused of egoism or arbitrariness or some other kind of immorality for thus thinking? I certainly can't see how.

Christian Belief Is Unjustified

This egoism objection, I think, is a nonstarter. A more important kind of objection here has it that Christian belief is *unjustified.* But what is this justification? What is it for a belief to be unjustified, or for a person to be unjustified in holding a certain belief?

THE DUAL NATURE OF JUSTIFICATION

There seem to be two strands to this notion of justification. On the one hand, justification seems to have something to do with *evidence:* a belief (or the believer) is unjustified if there isn't any evidence, or enough evidence, for that belief. On the other hand, justification seems to have something to do with *duty,* or *obligation,* or *moral rightness.* "Sam was entirely justified in rejecting his boss's harsh criticism"; this means, perhaps among other things, that Sam was within his rights, was contravening no duty, in rejecting his boss's harsh criticism.

If we take a look back in history to see where justification talk about belief originates, this two-strand appearance of justification is confirmed; we find concern with duty or obligation, and also with evidence. According to the important British philosopher John Locke (1632-1704) we have duties and obligations when it comes to what beliefs we form and hold. He asks this question: what are the ways in which "a rational creature, put in that state in which man is in this world, may and ought to govern

11

his opinions, and actions depending thereon?" In a classic text, he gives his answer: a rational creature in our circumstances ought to govern his opinions by *reason:*

> faith is nothing but a firm assent of the mind: which, if it be regulated, as is our duty, cannot be afforded to anything but upon good reason; and so cannot be opposite to it. He that believes without having any reason for believing, may be in love with his own fancies; but neither seeks truth as he ought, nor pays the obedience due to his Maker, who would have him use those discerning faculties he has given him, to keep him out of mistake and error. He that does not this to the best of his power, however he sometimes lights on truth, is in the right but by chance; and I know not whether the luckiness of the accident will excuse the irregularity of his proceeding. This at least is certain, that he must be accountable for whatever mistakes he runs into: whereas he that makes use of the light and faculties God has given him, and seeks sincerely to discover truth by those helps and abilities he has, may have this satisfaction in doing his duty as a rational creature, that, though he should miss truth, he will not miss the reward of it. For he governs his assent right, and places it as he should, who, in any case or matter whatsoever, believes or disbelieves according as reason directs him. He that doth otherwise, transgresses against his own light, and misuses those faculties which were given him to no other end, but to search and follow the clearer evidence and greater probability.[6]

Here Locke isn't speaking about specifically religious faith (faith as contrasted with reason, say), but about assent or opinion generally; and his central claim here is that there are duties and obligations with respect to its management or regulation. In particular, you are obliged to give assent only to that for which you have good reasons, good evidence. God commands us, says Locke, to seek truth in this way; he commands us to regulate our opinion in this way. If you don't follow this command, then you neither seek truth as you ought, nor pay due obedience to your maker. Someone who does seek truth in this way, even if he should happen to miss it, may still "have this satisfaction in doing his duty as a rational creature." You govern your assent "right," he says, you place it as you "should" if you

---

6. John Locke, *An Essay Concerning Human Understanding,* ed. A. D. Woozley (New York: World Publishing, 1963), IV.xvii.11.

believe or disbelieve as reason directs you. And if you don't do that, then you transgress against your own lights. One who governs his opinion thus is acting in accord with duty, is within his rights, is flouting no obligation, is not blameworthy, is, in a word, *justified.*[7]

So there are two strands to this notion of justification; on the one hand it has to do with duty and obligation; the idea is that there are duties and obligations with respect to what you believe and the way in which you believe. And this is the basic notion of justification: you are justified in believing something or other, in the basic sense, if you are fulfilling your obligations, not going contrary to duty in believing that thing. That's the first strand. According to the second strand, justification has to do with *evidence:* you are justified in believing some proposition just if you have sufficient evidence for that proposition. What is the connection between these two strands in Locke's thinking? Easy enough: Locke thinks the relevant duty is to believe only those propositions for which you have good evidence. We all have *this* duty: to believe a proposition only if we have sufficient evidence for it. So someone who believes that there is such a person as God but who doesn't know of evidence for that belief (arguments for the existence of God, for example) is going contrary to her duty and is therefore unjustified. The claim that Christian belief is unjustified (that the believer is unjustified) comes down to the claim that the believer doesn't have adequate evidence for this belief.

CLASSICAL FOUNDATIONALISM

Here there is a problem. The objector is evidently thinking of *propositional* evidence: evidence from other propositions one believes. The theistic arguments — cosmological, ontological, the argument from design, fine-tuning arguments — would be evidence of this sort for the existence of God, if indeed those arguments are good ones. And the objector is complaining that Christians don't have sufficient propositional evidence to support their beliefs.

7. The English terms 'justified', 'justification', and the like, go back at least to the King James translation of the Bible. We are justified, in this use, if Christ's atoning sacrifice for sin has applied to us, so that we are now no longer blameworthy and our sin has been covered, removed, obliterated, taken away; we are no longer guilty; it is as if (so far as guilt is concerned) our sin had never existed. This is close to the sense of 'justification' that Locke seems to have in mind.

But obviously you can't have propositional evidence for *everything* you believe. Every train of arguments will have to start somewhere, and the ultimate premises from which it starts will not themselves be believed on the evidential basis of other propositions; they will have to be accepted in the *basic* way, that is, not on the evidential basis of other beliefs. So presumably the objector is not holding that *every* belief, if it is to be justified, must be believed on the evidential basis of other beliefs; if that were true, no beliefs could be justified. (And if no beliefs could be justified, it is nothing in particular against religious beliefs if *they* can't be justified.) The objector must be supposing that some beliefs are *properly* basic: accepted in the basic way, not accepted on the evidential basis of other beliefs, and also such that one is *justified* in accepting them in that way.

John Locke was entirely aware of this. It was his idea that some beliefs are *certain;* and beliefs that are certain, he thought, can properly be accepted in the basic way. These certain beliefs fall into two kinds. First, some beliefs about my own mental life are certain. I believe I am in pain: that belief is certain for me. I believe, as I am looking out of the window, that there seem to be trees and grass and flowers there. I am certain of this: not that there *really are* trees and grass and flowers out there, but that it *looks to me* as if there are. We could call such beliefs "incorrigible": if you claim that you are in pain, or that it looks to you as if there is a tree there, I can't sensibly correct you and claim that you are mistaken. Incorrigible beliefs, according to Locke, are basic, and furthermore they are *properly* basic.

There is a second kind of belief that, according to Locke, is certain and therefore properly basic: *self-evident* beliefs. Examples would be beliefs like 2 + 2 = 4 or *Nothing can be red and green all over at the same time* or *If all men are mortal and Socrates is a man, then Socrates is mortal.* I can simply see that these beliefs are true. Such beliefs, we might say, are such that you can't understand them without seeing that they are true. So beliefs of these two kinds are properly basic; you can be justified in accepting them even if you don't believe them on the evidential basis of other beliefs you hold.

Think about the whole set of beliefs you hold. Locke thought of such a set of beliefs as having a characteristic structure: there are basic beliefs, which form the foundation of the structure, and there are nonbasic beliefs, which are accepted on the evidential basis of the basic beliefs. According to Locke, in a well-run, properly regulated set of beliefs, the only beliefs to be found in the foundation would be beliefs that are either self-evident or incorrigible. Locke's views here are an example of *classical foundation-alism,* as it is called. The classical foundationalist holds that the only sorts of beliefs that are properly basic are those of these two kinds: self-evident beliefs, and incorrigible beliefs. All other beliefs must be accepted on the basis of propositional evidence, that is, by way of arguments from other beliefs, arguments that trace back to those self-evident or incorrigible foundations.

Now Christian beliefs aren't just self-evident, like $2 + 1 = 3$, and neither, of course, are they just about one's own mental states. Therefore, according to the classical foundationalist, Christian beliefs must be accepted on the basis of arguments; they must be accepted on the evidential basis of other propositions. Thus one version of the claim that Christian belief is unjustified (that the believer is unjustified) arises out of classical foundationalism: it is really the claim that there is no good (or good enough) propositional evidence for Christian belief from propositions that are self-evident or incorrigible. Hence the Christian believer is unjustified; she is violating her epistemic duty.

But classical foundationalism itself has serious problems. First, it seems to shoot itself in the foot; it is hoist on its own petard; it is in self-referentially hot water. For according to classical foundationalism (hereafter, CF) you are within your epistemic rights in believing a proposition only if you believe it on the evidential basis of propositions that are self-evident or incorrigible.

If you believe a proposition for which there isn't any evidence from self-evident or incorrigible propositions, then you are unjustified and violating your epistemic duty. But here's the problem: there don't seem to be any incorrigible or self-evident propositions that support CF itself. It certainly isn't self-evident: it isn't such that anyone who understands it can just see it to be true. For example, I understand it, and I don't see it to be true. In fact I believe it is false. So it isn't *itself* self-evident; but it also looks as if there aren't any good arguments for CF from other propositions that are self-evident. Furthermore, CF isn't incorrigible; it isn't at all about how things appear or seem to anyone. Nor does it look as if there is a decent argument for CF from other propositions that are incorrigible. And still further, it certainly doesn't look as if there is a good argument for CF from propositions that are either self-evident or incorrigible. So, unless looks are deceiving here, even if CF is true, no one can properly believe CF; anyone who believes it is unjustified. Accordingly, CF seems to be self-referentially incoherent.

That's a serious problem, then, for the justificationist objection to Christian belief, at least if that objection is based on classical foundationalism. But the justificationist objector need not base her objection on classical foundationalism. Maybe she agrees with the classical foundationalist that Christian belief must be accepted on the basis of some evidence to be justified, but doesn't believe CF. Maybe she thinks that to be justified the Christian believer must have evidence from other things she believes, but doesn't necessarily need to have evidence from propositions that are self-evident or incorrigible. Then the above problem wouldn't affect her.

Still, there is another problem. According to the classical foundationalist, to be justified in believing, e.g., that there is a tree in my backyard, or that I see a tree in my backyard, I must believe that proposition on the evidence of propositions that are self-evident or incorrigible. Now maybe I can't find a decent argument of that sort for the proposition that there is a tree in my backyard. In fact maybe there *isn't* a decent argument of that sort for that proposition. I might try: "On most occasions in the past when it seemed to me that there was a tree in my backyard, there really was a tree there; on this occasion it seems to me that there is a tree there; so probably on this occasion there really is a tree there." But how do I know that on those past occasions when it seemed to me that there was a tree there, there really *was* a tree there? By appealing to *other* earlier past occasions? Clearly that's not going to work.

And what about the very idea of past occasions, or more generally what about the very idea of a past? I certainly believe that indeed there has been a past; but where can I find a good argument for the conclusion that there really *has* been a past? The whole development of modern philosophy from Descartes to Hume really shows that there is no good argument from what is self-evident or incorrigible to propositions of this sort.

Still, when I look out of my window, I do form the belief that there is a tree out there; and in fact it isn't within my power to withhold that belief. The fact is, beliefs of this sort are not under our voluntary control. We don't will to form them. It's not as if, when I look out into the backyard, I am appeared to in that familiar fashion, and then choose to believe that there is a tree there. I don't choose between believing this and not believing it: I just find myself believing. In the typical case, what I believe is not under my control; it really isn't up to me.

Perhaps in some special cases I decide what to believe — perhaps

16

I look at the evidence for some proposition, and then decide to believe it — but even in these cases it's not clear that this is what happens. What really does happen, so it seems to me, is that I decide to look at all the evidence; and when I do, either I find the evidence convincing to one degree or another, whereupon I believe the proposition in question or think it likely, or I don't find the evidence convincing, and don't believe the proposition. But I really don't tot up the evidence and then just *decide* whether or not to believe.

If so, however, moral categories — duty and obligation, etc. — don't really apply to beliefs (believings). Go back to my belief that there is a tree there: under the circumstances in question it just isn't up to me whether or not I form that belief; I simply find myself with it. But then how could I be going contrary to duty in holding that belief? If I fell out of an airplane at 3,000 feet, I would fall down, not up; and it wouldn't be up to me which way I fell. But then I couldn't be going contrary to my duty in falling down; my falling down isn't something that can be morally evaluated; I can't sensibly be either praised or blamed for falling down. And isn't it the same with respect to belief? If it isn't within my power to withhold belief, in those circumstances, then in those circumstances I couldn't be going contrary to my duty; therefore in those circumstances I couldn't be unjustified. And isn't the same thing true for religious belief? I am a theist; I believe that there is such a person as God; but I have never *decided* to hold this belief. It has always just seemed to me to be true. And it isn't as if I could rid myself of this belief just by an act of will.

JUSTIFICATION WITHOUT EVIDENCE

In any event, it is perfectly plain that someone could be justified in accepting the whole Christian story; that is, it is plain that someone could accept that story without going contrary to duty. It isn't at all difficult for a Christian — even a sophisticated, and knowledgeable contemporary believer aware of all the criticisms and contrary currents of opinion — to be justified, in this sense, in her belief; and this whether or not she believes in God (or in more specific Christian doctrines) on the basis of propositional evidence. For consider such a believer. She is aware of the objections people have made to Christian belief; she has read and reflected on Freud, Marx, and Nietzsche (not to mention Flew, Mackie, and Nielsen) and the other critics of Christian or theistic belief; she knows that the world contains many who do not believe as she does. She doesn't believe on the basis of propositional evidence; she therefore believes in the basic way. Can she be justified in believing in God in this way?

The answer seems to be pretty easy. She reads Nietzsche, but remains unmoved by his complaint that Christianity fosters a weak, whining, whimpering, pusillanimous, duplicitous, and generally disgusting kind of person: most of the Christians she knows or knows of — Mother Teresa, for example — don't fit that mold. She finds Freud's contemptuous attitude towards Christianity and theistic belief backed by little more than implausible fantasies about the origin of belief in God (patricide in the primal horde?[8] Can he be serious?); and she finds little more of substance in Marx. She thinks as carefully as she can about these objections and others, but finds them wholly uncompelling.

On the other side, although she is aware of theistic arguments and thinks some of them not without value, she doesn't believe on the basis of them. Rather, she has a rich inner spiritual life, the sort described in the early pages of Jonathan Edwards's *Religious Affections;*[9] it seems to her that she is sometimes made aware, catches a glimpse, of something of the overwhelming beauty and loveliness of the Lord; she is often aware, as it strongly seems to her, of the work of the Holy Spirit in her heart, comforting, encouraging, teaching, leading her to accept the "great things of the gospel" (as Edwards calls them), helping her see that the magnificent scheme of salvation devised by the Lord himself is not only for others but for her as well.

After long, hard, conscientious reflection, this all seems to her enormously more convincing than the complaints of the critics. Is she then going contrary to duty in believing as she does? Is she being irresponsible? Clearly not. There could be something *defective* about her, some malfunction not apparent on the surface. She could be *mistaken,* a victim of illusion or wishful thinking despite her best efforts. She could be wrong, desperately wrong, pitiably wrong, in thinking these things; nevertheless she isn't flouting any discernible duty. She is fulfilling her epistemic responsibilities; she is doing her level best; she is justified.

And this is not only true, but *obviously* true. We may feel in some

8. See below, p. 21, and see Freud's "An Autobiographical Study," in Volume 20 of the *Standard Edition of the Complete Psychological Works of Sigmund Freud*, 24 vols. (London: Hogarth Press and the Institute of Psychoanalysis, 1953-74), p. 68.

9. *A Treatise Concerning Religious Affections,* ed. John E. Smith (New Haven: Yale University Press, 1959 [1746]), p. 271.

subterranean way that without evidence she isn't justified; if so, this must be because we are importing some other conception of justification. But if it is justification in the deontological sense, the sense involving responsibility, being within one's intellectual rights, she is surely justified. For how could she possibly be blameworthy or irresponsible, if she thinks about the matter as hard as she can, in the most responsible way she can, and still comes to these conclusions?

Indeed, no matter *what* conclusions she arrived at, wouldn't she be justified if she arrived at them in this way? Even if they are wholly unreasonable? A patient at Pine Rest Christian Psychiatric Hospital in Cutlerville, Michigan, once complained that he wasn't getting the credit he deserved for inventing a new form of human reproduction, "rotational reproduction" as he called it. This kind of reproduction doesn't involve sex. Instead, you suspend a woman from the ceiling with a rope and get her rotating at a high rate of speed; the result is a large number of children, enough to populate a city the size of Chicago. As a matter of fact, he claimed, this is precisely how Chicago *was* populated. He realized, he said, that there is something churlish about insisting on getting all the credit due one, but he did think he really hadn't got enough recognition for this important discovery. After all, where would Chicago be without it?

Now there is no reason to think this unfortunate man was flouting epistemic duty, or derelict with respect to cognitive requirement, or careless about his epistemic obligations, or cognitively irresponsible. Perhaps he was doing his level best to satisfy these obligations. Indeed, we can imagine that his main goal, in life, is satisfying his intellectual obligations and carrying out his cognitive duties. Perhaps he was dutiful *in excelsis*. If so, he was *justified* in these insane beliefs, even if they are insane, and even if they result from cognitive dysfunction.

Christian Belief Is Irrational

Granted: this man need not be flouting duty; he is or may be justified. Still, there is obviously something seriously wrong with his whole belief structure. It isn't just that his beliefs are false; they are also in a clear sense *irrational*. In what sense? According to Aristotle, man is a rational animal. That is, human beings, unlike, say, bacteria, have *reason;* they can think, form beliefs, learn about their environments, use arguments of various sorts, and the like. Now suppose we think of reason as something like a faculty or power by virtue of which human beings are able to do these things. Like other faculties, reason can sometimes fail to function properly; it can malfunction. And one way in which it can malfunction is by way of producing bizarre beliefs, as with the above advocate of rotational reproduction.

Of course reason, this faculty, produces different beliefs in different circumstances. Upon looking out of the window, I form the belief that I see a bunch of blackbirds in the backyard; upon attending a concert, I may form the belief that the brass is too loud. These beliefs would be perfectly proper in those circumstances. But if at the concert I form the belief that I see a bunch of blackbirds in the backyard, or if when looking out of the window I form the belief that the brass is too loud, then something has gone wrong — my cognitive powers are misfiring or malfunctioning; my beliefs, in those circumstances, are irrational. More generally, we could say that a belief is irrational, in given circumstances, if in those circumstances someone whose cognitive powers were *functioning properly,* not subject to malfunction, would not form that belief. A belief is rational, in given circumstances, if someone whose cognitive powers are functioning properly, could form that belief in those circumstances. According to this definition, that belief in rotational reproduction is irrational.

But what about Christian belief? Can Christian belief be held by someone whose cognitive faculties are functioning properly? This question, I think, brings us closer to a viable *de jure* criticism of Christian belief. So far we've seen several failed candidates for a viable *de jure* criticism: that Christian belief is arbitrary or egotistical, that Christian belief can't be justified, that it is wanting because there aren't good arguments for it, and so on. And what we've seen, so far, is that these objections don't really hold water. But with this question about rationality, we get closer to a defensible *de jure* criticism of Christian belief. Here we can properly start, I think, by considering the sort of objection offered by Karl Marx (1818-1883) and Sigmund Freud (1856-1939), those great "masters of suspicion" as they are sometimes called. These objections are crucially related to the question of *warrant,* that property or quality which distinguishes knowledge from mere true belief. We'll get to warrant in a bit: right now, we'll take a look at the objections offered by Marx and Freud.

Marx doesn't have a great deal to say about religion, but what he does say can hardly be considered complimentary:

> The basis of irreligious criticism is *man makes religion,* religion does not make man. In other words, religion is the self-consciousness and

the self-feeling of the man who has either not yet found himself, or else (having found himself) has lost himself once more. But man is no abstract being squatting outside the world. Man is *the world of man,* the state, society. This state, this society, produce religion, *a perverted world consciousness,* because they are a *perverted* world. . . .

Religious distress is at the same time the *expression* of real distress and the *protest* against real distress. Religion is the sigh of the oppressed creature, the heart of a heartless world, just as it is the spirit of a spiritless situation. It is the *opium* of the people.

The abolition of religion as the *illusory* happiness of the people is required for their *real* happiness. The demand to give up the illusions about its condition is the *demand to give up a condition which requires illusions.* The criticism of religion is therefore *in embryo the criticism of the vale of woe,* the *halo* of which is religion.[10]

Marx's idea is that religion arises from a *perverted* world-consciousness. Religious belief is both a result and a manifestation of cognitive malfunction or dysfunction, a lack of mental and/or emotional health. This cognitive dysfunction is due to social dysfunction; because she is living in a dysfunctional, perverse social environment, the believer's cognitive powers aren't functioning properly; they aren't functioning in a healthy fashion. If her cognitive equipment *were* working properly — if, for example, it were working more like Marx's — she would not be under the spell of this illusion. She would instead face the world and our place in it with the clear-eyed apprehension that we are alone, and that any comfort and help we get will have to be of our own devising.

Freud's criticism is different in an interesting way. There are several sides to Freud's critique of religion; for one thing he was fascinated by what he saw as the Darwinian picture of early human beings living in packs or herds, all the females belonging to one powerful, dominant jealous male; one day his sons, smarting under the condition that all the women belonged to their father, "came together and united to overwhelm, kill and devour their father, who had been their enemy, but also their ideal."[11] Their remorse and guilt, Freud thinks, are one source of religion.

10. "Contribution to the Critique of Hegel's Philosophy of Right," in Karl Marx and Friedrich Engels, *On Religion,* ed. Reinhold Niebuhr (Chico, CA: Scholar's Press, 1964), pp. 41-42. Emphasis is in the original. Engels substantially echoes Marx's remarks.

11. See above, note 8.

Well, perhaps this grisly little tale doesn't come to much as a serious contribution to the history of religion. Freud's most characteristic criticism looks in a different direction. We noted above the insane beliefs of the advocate of rotational reproduction (above, p. 19); these beliefs, of course, were due to cognitive malfunction. There are more subtle ways, however, in which non-rational or irrational beliefs can be formed in us. Note first that there are belief-forming processes or mechanisms that are aimed, not at the formation of true belief, but at the formation of belief with some other property — the property of contributing to survival, perhaps, or to peace of mind, or psychological well-being.[12] Someone with a lethal disease may believe his chances for recovery much higher than the statistics in his possession would warrant; the processes that produce such belief are not aimed at furnishing true beliefs, but at furnishing beliefs that make it more likely that the believer will recover. A mountaineer whose survival depends on his ability to leap a crevasse (it's getting dark and cold and he doesn't have survival gear with him) may form an extremely optimistic estimate of his powers as a long-jumper; it is more likely that he will be able to leap the crevasse (or at least give it a try) if he thinks he can, than if he thinks he can't. Most of us form estimates of our intelligence, wisdom, and moral fiber that are considerably higher than an objective estimate would warrant; no doubt nine out of ten of us think ourselves well above average along these lines.

Furthermore a person may be blinded (as we say) by ambition, failing to see that a certain course of action is wrong or stupid, even though it is obvious to everyone else. Our idea, here, is that the inordinately ambitious man fails to recognize something he would otherwise recognize; the normal functioning of some aspect of his cognitive powers is inhibited or overridden or impeded by that excessive ambition. You may be blinded also by loyalty, continuing to believe in the honesty of your friend long after an objective look at the evidence would have dictated a reluctant change

---

12. This from John Locke:

> Would it not be an insufferable thing for a learned professor, and that which his scarlet would blush at, to have his authority of forty years standing wrought out of hard rock Greek and Latin, with no small expence of time and candle, and confirmed by general tradition, and a reverent beard, in an instant overturned by an upstart novelist? Can any one expect that he should be made to confess, that what he taught his scholars thirty years ago, was all errour and mistake; and that he sold them hard words and ignorance at a very dear rate? (*Essay Concerning Human Understanding*, IV.xx.11)

of mind. You can also be blinded by covetousness, love, fear, lust, anger, pride, grief, social pressure, and a thousand other things. In polemic, it is common to attack someone's views by claiming that the denial of what they think is patently obvious (i.e., such that any right thinking, properly functioning person can immediately see that it is so); we then attribute their opposing this obvious truth either to dishonesty (they don't really believe what they say [after all, who could?]) or to their being blinded by something or other — maybe a reluctance to change, an aversion to new ideas, personal ambition, sexism, racism, homophobia, and so on.

In a similar vein, Richard Dawkins insists that "It is absolutely safe to say that if you meet someone who claims not to believe in evolution, that person is ignorant, stupid or insane (or wicked, but I'd rather not consider that)."[13] Dawkins apparently thinks the truth of evolution is utterly clear and obvious to anyone who is not unduly ignorant, is not too stupid to follow the arguments, and is sane, i.e., such that her rational faculties are functioning properly; it is therefore so obvious that any person who wasn't just (wickedly) lying through her teeth would have to admit that she believes in evolution. What are appealed to in all these cases are mechanisms that can override or cancel what our rational faculties would ordinarily deliver.

What we see, therefore, is that there are at least two ways in which a belief can be irrational: it may be produced by malfunctioning faculties, or by cognitive processes aimed at something other than the truth. This brings us to Freud's best-known account of the psychological origins of belief in God:

> These [religious beliefs], which are given out as teachings, are not precipitates of experience or end-results of thinking: they are illusions, fulfillments of the oldest, strongest and most urgent wishes of mankind. The secret of their strength lies in the strength of those wishes. As we already know, the terrifying impressions of helplessness in childhood aroused the need for protection — for protection through love — which was provided by the father; and the recognition that

13. *New York Times* (April 9, 1989), sec. 7, p. 34. Daniel Dennett goes Dawkins one (or two) better, claiming that one who so much as harbors doubts about evolution is "inexcusably ignorant" (*Darwin's Dangerous Idea* [New York: Simon & Schuster, 1995], p. 46) — thus displaying *both* ignorance *and* wrong-doing. You wake up in the middle of the night; you think about that whole vast and sweeping evolutionary account; you ask yourself: "Can it really be true?" Bam! You are inexcusably ignorant!

this helplessness lasts throughout life made it necessary to cling to the existence of a father, but this time a more powerful one. Thus the benevolent rule of a divine Providence allays our fear of the dangers of life; the establishment of a moral world-order ensures the fulfillment of the demands of justice, which have so often remained unfulfilled in human civilization; and the prolongation of earthly existence in a future life provides the local and temporal framework in which these wish-fulfillments shall take place.[14]

Freud's idea is that belief in God arises from a psychological mechanism he calls 'wish-fulfillment' or wishful thinking; nature rises up against us, cold, pitiless, implacable, blind to our needs and desires. She delivers hurt, fear, and pain; and in the end she demands our death. Paralyzed and appalled, we invent (unconsciously, of course) a Father in Heaven who exceeds our earthly fathers as much in power and knowledge as in goodness and benevolence; the alternative would be to sink into depression, stupor, paralysis, and finally death. So according to Freud, belief in God is an *illusion:* a belief that arises from the mechanism of wish-fulfillment.[15] An illusion isn't necessarily false; but Freud thinks this illusion is one we can resist, and that it is intellectually irresponsible not to resist it:

> If there was ever a case of a lame excuse we have it here. Ignorance is ignorance: no right to believe anything can be derived from it. In other matters no sensible person will behave so irresponsibly or rest content with such feeble grounds for his opinions and for the lines he takes. . . . Where questions of religion are concerned, people are guilty of every possible sort of dishonesty and intellectual misdemeanor.[16]

Once we see that religious belief takes its origin in wishful thinking, we will presumably no longer find it attractive; perhaps this will also, as in his case, induce in us a certain pity for those benighted souls who will never rise to our enlightened heights:

14. *The Future of an Illusion,* trans. and ed. James Strachey (New York and London: Norton, 1961), p. 30. This work was originally published as *Die Zukunft einer Illusion* (Leipzig and Zurich: Internationaler Psychoanalytischer Verlag, 1927).

15. And in such a way that it (or its deliverances) rather resembles Calvin's *sensus divinitatis* (Chapter Three below); see also Freud's *Moses and Monotheism* (New York: Vintage, 1939), pp. 167ff.

16. *Future of an Illusion,* p. 32.

The whole thing is so patently infantile, so incongruous with reality, that to one whose attitude to humanity is friendly, it is painful to think that the great majority of mortals will never be able to rise above this view of life.[17]

Freud and Marx both criticize religion, but in interestingly different ways. Marx's claim is that religious belief arises from cognitive dysfunction; as a result of living in a dysfunctional society the believer's cognitive faculties are not working properly. Freud, on the other hand, doesn't claim that the believer is suffering from cognitive malfunction. Belief in God is an illusion, he says, but illusion has its uses, in particular in enabling us to live in this cold, bleak, miserable world in which we find ourselves. Someone with properly functioning cognitive faculties might very well form religious belief. Still, there is a problem with such belief: it isn't produced by cognitive faculties whose purpose is to furnish us with true beliefs about our world. Perception is a faculty whose purpose it is to give us true belief. The same is not true for wish-fulfillment, however; the purpose of wish-fulfillment is instead to enable us to get along in a hostile or indifferent world. And it does so by projecting an unseen father into the heavens, a father who really does care for us and has our best interests at heart.

Warrant and the F&M Complaint

Freud and Marx (F&M) lead us to a more promising version of the *de jure* criticism: it is that religious belief — belief in God, for example — lacks *warrant*. I'll use the term 'warrant' as a name of the property that distinguishes knowledge from mere true belief. And since that property comes in degrees, we'll have to put it like this: *warrant is the property enough of which is what distinguishes knowledge from mere true belief.* It's pretty obvious that you can have a true belief that isn't a case of knowledge. You have travelled 2,000 miles to the North Cascades for a climbing trip; you are desperately eager to climb. Being an incurable optimist, you believe it will be bright, sunny, and warm tomorrow, despite the forecast, which calls for high winds and a nasty mixture of rain, sleet, and snow. As it turns out, the forecasters were wrong and tomorrow turns out sunny and beautiful:

17. *Civilization and Its Discontents,* trans. Joan Riviere (London: Hogarth Press, 1949), p. 23.

your belief was true, but didn't constitute knowledge. What is needed, in addition to truth, for a belief to be knowledge? I'll use the term 'warrant' to name that property, whatever it is.

1. Proper Function

My suggestion begins with the idea that a belief has warrant only if it is produced by cognitive faculties that are *functioning properly,* subject to no disorder or dysfunction. The notion of proper function is fundamental to our central ways of thinking about knowledge.

But that notion is inextricably bound with another: that of a *design plan.* Human beings and their organs are so constructed that there is a way they *should* work, a way they are *supposed* to work, a way they work when they work right; this is the way they work when there is no malfunction. There is a way in which your heart is supposed to work: for example, your pulse rate should be about 50-80 beats per minute when you are at rest, and (if you are under 40) achieve a maximum rate of some 180-200 beats per minute when you are exercising really hard. If your resting pulse is 160, or if you can't get your pulse above 60 beats per minute no matter how hard you work, then your heart isn't functioning properly. (On the other hand, a mallard whose resting heart rate is 160 might be perfectly healthy.)

We needn't initially take the notions of *design plan* and the *way in which a thing is supposed to work* to entail *conscious* design or purpose. I don't here mean to claim that organisms are created by a conscious agent (God) according to a design plan, in something like the way in which human artifacts are constructed and designed. I am not supposing, initially at least, that having a design plan implies having been created by God or some other conscious agent.[18] I mean instead to point to something nearly all of us, theists or not, in fact believe: there is a way in which a human organ or system works when it works properly, works as it is supposed to work; and this way of working is given by its design or design plan.

Proper function and design go hand in hand with the notion of *purpose.* The various organs and systems of the body (and the ways in which they work) have their purposes: the function or purpose of the heart is to pump the blood; of the immune system, to fight off disease;

18. Although in *Warrant and Proper Function* (New York: Oxford University Press, 1993), chap. 11, I argue that there is no viable naturalistic account of proper function.

of the lungs, to provide oxygen; and so on. If the design is a *good* design, then when the organ or system functions properly, i.e., according to its design plan, that purpose will be achieved. Of course the design plan for human beings will include specifications for our *cognitive* system or faculties, as well as for noncognitive systems and organs. Like the rest of our organs and systems, our cognitive faculties can work well or ill; they can malfunction or function properly. They too work in a certain way when they are functioning properly — and work in a certain way to accomplish their purpose. Accordingly, the first element in our conception of warrant (so I say) is that a belief has warrant for someone only if her faculties are functioning properly, are subject to no relevant dysfunction, in producing that belief.

2. Correct Environment

Many systems of your body, obviously, are designed to work *in a certain kind of environment.* You can't breathe under water; your muscles atrophy in zero gravity; you can't get enough oxygen at the top of Mt. Everest. Clearly the same goes for your cognitive faculties; they too will achieve their purpose only if functioning in an environment much like the one for which they were designed (by God or evolution). Thus they won't work well in an environment (on some other planet, for example) in which a certain subtle radiation impedes the function of memory.

3. Aimed at True Belief

But this is not enough. It is clearly possible that a belief be produced by cognitive faculties that are functioning properly in an environment for which they were designed, but nonetheless lack warrant; the above two conditions are not sufficient. We think that the purpose or function of our belief-producing faculties is that of furnishing us with true (or verisimilitudinous) belief. As we saw above in connection with the Freud and Marx complaint, however, it is clearly possible that the purpose or function of *some* belief-producing faculties or mechanisms is the production of beliefs with some other virtue — perhaps that of enabling us to get along in this cold, cruel, threatening world, or of enabling us to survive a dangerous situation or a life-threatening disease. So we must add that the belief in question is produced by cognitive faculties whose *purpose* is that of producing true belief.

4. Successfully *Aimed at True Belief*

Even this isn't sufficient. We can see why by reflecting on a fantasy of David Hume's:

> This world, for aught he knows, is very faulty and imperfect, compared to a superior standard; and was only the first rude essay of some infant Deity, who afterwards abandoned it, ashamed of his lame performance; it is the work only of some dependent, inferior Deity; and is the object of derision to his superiors: it is the production of old age and dotage in some superannuated Deity; and ever since his death, has run on at adventures, from the first impulse and active force, which it received from him.[19]

So imagine that a young and untutored apprentice deity sets out to build cognitive beings, beings capable of belief and knowledge. Immaturity and incompetence triumph; the design contains serious glitches. In fact, in some area of the design, when the faculties work just as they were designed to, the result is ludicrously false belief: thus when the cognitive faculties of these beings are working according to their design plan, they constantly confuse horses and hearses, forming the odd beliefs that cowboys in the old west rode hearses and that corpses are usually transported in horses. These beliefs are then produced by cognitive faculties working properly in the right sort of environment according to a design plan aimed at truth, but they still lack warrant. What is missing? Clearly enough, what must be added is that the design plan in question is a *good* one, one that is *successfully* aimed at truth, one such that there is a high probability that a belief produced according to that plan will be true (or nearly true).

Put in a nutshell, then, *a belief has warrant for a person S only if that belief is produced in S by cognitive faculties functioning properly (subject to no dysfunction) in a cognitive environment that is appropriate for S's kind of cognitive faculties, according to a design plan that is successfully aimed at truth.*

---

19. *Dialogues Concerning Natural Religion,* ed. Nelson Pike (Indianapolis and New York: Bobbs-Merrill, 1970), p. 53.

Back to the F&M Complaint

Now we are ready to return to the F&M complaint: this complaint is really the claim that theistic belief *lacks warrant*. According to Freud, theistic belief is produced by cognitive faculties that are functioning properly, but the process that produces it — wishful thinking — does not have the production of true belief as its purpose; it is aimed instead at something like enabling us to carry on in the grim and threatening world in which we find ourselves. Therefore theistic belief does not meet the third condition of warrant. Theistic belief is no more respectable, epistemically speaking, than propositions selected entirely at random. It is baseless superstition.

Marx's views are similar. He thinks first that theistic and religious belief is produced by cognitive faculties that are not functioning properly. Those faculties are dysfunctional; and the dysfunction is due to a sort of perversion in social structure, a sort of social malfunction. Therefore religious belief doesn't meet the first condition of warrant; therefore it is without warrant, and an intellectually healthy person will reject it. Further, Marx also thinks that a person whose cognitive faculties are functioning properly and who knows what was known by the middle of the nineteenth century will see that materialism is very probably true, in which case Christian and theistic belief is very likely false. So he would join Freud in the contention that Christian and theistic belief is without warrant, a baseless superstition, and very probably false.

Marx and Freud, therefore, complain that religious belief is irrational; their complaint is best construed as the claim that religious belief lacks warrant. In the next chapter we'll look into this claim.

CHAPTER THREE

Warranted Belief in God

*. . . For since the creation of the world God's invisible qualities
— his eternal power and divine nature — have been clearly seen,
being understood from what has been made.*

St. Paul

Not enough evidence, God! Not enough evidence!

Bertrand Russell

The *de jure* challenge to Christian (or theistic) belief, as we have seen, is
the claim that such belief is irrational, or unreasonable, or unjustified, or
in some other way properly subject to unfriendly epistemic criticism; it
contrasts with the *de facto* challenge, according to which the belief in question is false. What we saw in the last chapter is that this *de jure* complaint
is best understood as the claim that Christian and other theistic belief is
irrational in the sense that it originates in cognitive malfunction (Marx)
or in cognitive proper function that is aimed at something other than the
truth (Freud) — comfort, perhaps, or the ability to soldier on in this appalling world in which we find ourselves. To put it another way, the claim is
that such belief doesn't originate in cognitive faculties that are functioning
properly in a suitable environment according to a design plan successfully
aimed at producing true beliefs. To put it in still another way, the charge
is that theistic and Christian belief *lacks warrant*.

By way of response, in this chapter I shall first offer a model — a
model based on a claim made jointly by Thomas Aquinas and John Calvin

— for a way in which theistic belief could have warrant. Once we see that and how theistic belief might have warrant, we can also see the futility of the F&M complaint and its contemporary successors. In the next chapter I'll extend the model to cover specifically Christian belief.

The A/C Model

To give a *model* of a proposition, as I'm thinking of it, is to exhibit a possible state of affairs in which that proposition is true, thus showing how it could be true. So I'll be trying to show how theistic belief, contrary to what Freud and Marx say, could have warrant. And here I'll be following both Thomas Aquinas and John Calvin; hence, the 'A/C model.' Aquinas and Calvin agree on the claim that there is a kind of natural knowledge of God (and who can reject anything on which Calvin and Aquinas are in accord?). My model is based on Calvin's version of the suggestion, not because I think Calvin is to be preferred to Aquinas, but because we can usefully see his suggestion as a kind of meditation on and development of a theme suggested by Aquinas.

According to Aquinas, "To know in a general and confused way that God exists is implanted in us by nature."[1] In the opening chapters of the *Institutes of the Christian Religion*[2] Calvin concurs: there is a sort of natural knowledge of God. Calvin expands this theme into a suggestion as to how beliefs about God can have warrant and constitute knowledge. What he says can be seen as a development of that remark of Thomas Aquinas's; but it can also be seen as a development of what the apostle Paul says in Romans 1:

> For the wrath of God is revealed from heaven against all ungodliness and wickedness of men who by their wickedness suppress the truth. For what can be known about God is plain to them, because God has shown it to them. Ever since the creation of the world his invisible nature, namely, his eternal power and deity, has been clearly per-

1. *Summa Theologiae* I, q. 2 a. 1, ad 1. In *Summa Contra Gentiles* Aquinas adds that "There is a certain general and confused knowledge of God, which is in almost all men" (Bk. III, ch. 38).

2. Ed. John T. McNeill and trans. Ford Lewis Battles (Philadelphia: Westminster, 1960 [1559]). Page references to the *Institutes* are to this edition.

ceived in the things that have been made. So they are without excuse. (Rom. 1:18-20 RSV)[3]

For our purposes, Calvin's basic claim is that there is a sort of a natural instinctive human tendency, a disposition to form beliefs about God under a variety of conditions and in a variety of situations. In his commentary on the above passage:

> By saying that God has made it manifest, he means that man was created to be a spectator of this formed world, and that eyes were given him, that he might, by looking on so beautiful a picture, be led up to the Author himself.[4]

In the *Institutes* he develops this thought:

> There is within the human mind, and indeed by natural instinct, an awareness of divinity. This we take to be beyond controversy. To prevent anyone from taking refuge in the pretense of ignorance, God himself has implanted in all men a certain understanding of his divine majesty. . . . Since, therefore, men one and all perceive that there is a God and that he is their Maker, they are condemned by their own testimony because they have failed to honor him and to consecrate their lives to his will. . . . there is, as the eminent pagan [i.e., Cicero] says, no nation so barbarous, no people so savage, that they have not a deep-seated conviction that there is a God. . . . Therefore, since from the beginning of the world there has been no region, no city, in short, no household, that could do without religion, there lies in this a tacit confession of a sense of deity inscribed in the hearts of all. (*Institutes* I.iii.1, pp. 43-44)

3. As Etienne Gilson says, very many medieval and later thinkers have found in this passage a charter for natural theology, construed as the effort to present proofs or arguments for the existence of God. But is Paul really talking here about proofs or arguments? Natural theology, as Aquinas says, is pretty difficult for most of us; most of us have neither the leisure, ability, inclination nor education to follow those theistic proofs. But here Paul seems to be speaking of *all* of us human beings; what can be known about God is *plain*, he says. It is true that this knowledge comes by way of what God has made, but it doesn't follow that it comes by way of *argument*, the arguments of natural theology, for example.

4. *Commentaries on the Epistle of Paul the Apostle to the Romans*, Volume 19 of *Calvin's Commentaries* (Grand Rapids: Baker Book House Co., 1979; originally printed for the Calvin Translation Society of Edinburgh, Scotland), p. 70.

Calvin goes on to claim that many rejections of God, or attempts to do without him, are really further testimonies to this natural inclination:

> Indeed, the perversity of the impious, who though they struggle furiously are unable to extricate themselves from the fear of God, is abundant testimony that this conviction, namely, that there is some God, is naturally inborn in all, and is fixed deep within, as it were in the very marrow. . . . From this we conclude that it is not a doctrine that must first be learned in school, but one of which each of us is master from his mother's womb and which nature itself permits no one to forget, although many strive with every nerve to this end. (I.iii.3, p. 46)

I'll take Calvin as suggesting that there is a kind of faculty (like sight or hearing) or a cognitive mechanism — what he calls a *"sensus divinitatis"* or sense of divinity — which in a wide variety of circumstances produces in us beliefs about God. These circumstances trigger the disposition to form the beliefs in question; they form the occasion on which those beliefs arise. Under these circumstances we develop or form theistic beliefs. More exactly, these beliefs are *formed in us* in those circumstances; in the typical case we don't consciously choose to have those beliefs. Instead, we find ourselves with them, just as we find ourselves with perceptual and memory beliefs. (You don't and can't simply *decide* to have this belief, thereby acquiring it.[5]) These passages suggest that awareness of God is natural, widespread, and not easy to forget, ignore, or destroy. Seventy years of determined but unsuccessful Marxist efforts to uproot Christianity in the former Soviet Union tend to confirm this claim.[6]

It sounds as if Calvin thinks knowledge of God is *innate,* and hence such that one has it from the time he is born, "from his mother's womb." Still, perhaps Calvin doesn't really mean to endorse the idea that, say, a one-year-old has this knowledge. The *capacity* for such knowledge is indeed innate, but a bit of maturity is required before it actually shows up. The capacity for arithmetical knowledge is innate; still, it doesn't follow that we know elementary arithmetic from our mother's womb; it takes

---

5. See my "Reason and Belief in God," in *Faith and Rationality,* ed. A. Plantinga and Nicholas Wolterstorff (Notre Dame: University of Notre Dame Press, 1983), pp. 34ff.

6. It is no part of the model, however, to hold that the *sensus divinitatis* is never subject to malfunction; perhaps it is sometimes diseased or even inoperative. It can also be impeded in the usual ways, and its deliverances can perhaps sometimes be extinguished by the wrong kind of nurture.

a little maturity. My guess is Calvin thinks the same with respect to this knowledge of God; what one has from his mother's womb is not this knowledge of God, but a capacity for it. Whatever Calvin thinks, however, it's my model; and according to the model the development of the *sensus divinitatis* requires a certain maturity (although it is indeed sometimes manifested by very young children).

You see the blazing glory of the heavens from a mountainside at 13,000 feet; you think about those unimaginable distances; you find yourself filled with awe and wonder — and also with the belief that God must indeed be great to have created this magnificent heavenly host. But it isn't only the variety of the heavenly host that catches Calvin's eye here:

> Lest anyone, then, be excluded from access to happiness, he not only sowed in men's minds that seed of religion of which we have spoken, but revealed himself and daily discloses himself in the whole workmanship of the universe. As a consequence, men cannot open their eyes without being compelled to see him. . . . But upon his individual works he has engraved unmistakable marks of his glory. . . . wherever you cast your eyes, there is no spot in the universe wherein you cannot discern at least some sparks of his glory. (I.v.i, p. 52)[7]

Calvin's idea is that the workings of the *sensus divinitatis* are triggered or occasioned by a wide variety of circumstances, including in particular some of the glories of nature: the marvelous, impressive beauty of the night sky; the timeless crash and roar of the surf that resonates deep within us; the majestic grandeur of the mountains (the North Cascades, say, as viewed from Whatcom Pass); the ancient, brooding presence of the Australian outback; the thunder of a great waterfall. But it isn't only grandeur and majesty that counts; he would say the same for the subtle play of sunlight on a field in spring, or the dainty, articulate beauty of a tiny flower, or aspen leaves shimmering and dancing in the breeze: "there is no spot in the universe," he says, "wherein you cannot discern at least some sparks of his glory."

Calvin could have added other sorts of circumstances: there is some-

---

7. Compare Charles Sanders Peirce: "A man looks upon nature, sees its sublimity and beauty, and his spirit gradually rises to the idea of God. He does not see the Divinity, nor does nature prove to him the existence of that Being, but it does excite his mind and imagination until the idea becomes rooted in his heart." Quoted by Edward T. Oakes, "Discovering the American Aristotle," *First Things* (Dec. 1993): 27.

thing like an awareness of divine disapproval upon having done what is wrong, or cheap, and something like a perception of divine forgiveness upon confession and repentance. People in grave danger instinctively turn to the Lord, asking for succor and support. (They say there are no atheists in foxholes.) On a beautiful spring morning (the birds singing, heaven and earth alight and alive with glory, the air fresh and cool, the treetops gleaming in the sun) a spontaneous hymn of thanks to the Lord — thanks for your circumstances and your very existence — may arise in your soul. According to the model, therefore, there are many circumstances, and circumstances of many different kinds, that call forth or occasion theistic belief.

Basicality

According to the A/C model, this natural knowledge of God is not arrived at by inference or argument (for example the famous theistic proofs of natural theology) but in a much more immediate way. The deliverances of the *sensus divinitatis* are not quick inferences from the circumstances that trigger its operation. It isn't that one beholds the night sky, notes that it is grand, and concludes that there must be such a person as God: as an argument, this would be pretty weak. It isn't that one notes some feature of the Australian outback — that it is ancient and brooding, for example — and draws the conclusion that God exists. It is rather that upon the perception of the night sky or the mountain vista or the tiny flower these beliefs just arise within us. They *arise* in these circumstances; they are not conclusions from them. The heavens declare the glory of God and the skies proclaim the work of his hands (Psalm 19): but not by way of serving as premises for an argument.

In this regard the *sensus divinitatis* resembles the faculties of perception, memory, and *a priori* knowledge. Consider the first. I look out into the backyard; I see that the coral tiger lilies are in bloom. I don't note that I am being appeared to in a certain complicated way (that my experience is of a certain complicated character) and then make an argument from my being appeared to in that way to the conclusion that in fact there are coral tiger lilies in bloom there. (The whole history of modern philosophy up to Hume and Reid shows how inconclusive such an argument would be.) It is rather that upon being appeared to in that way (and given my previous training), the belief that the coral tiger lilies are in bloom spontaneously arises in me. This belief will ordinarily be *basic,* in the sense that it is not accepted on the evidential basis of other propositions. The same goes for memory. You ask me what I had for breakfast; I think for a moment and then remember: pancakes with blueberries. I don't argue from the fact that it *seems* to me that I remember having pancakes for breakfast to the conclusion that in fact I did; rather, you ask me what I had for breakfast and the answer simply comes to mind.

Proper Basicality with Respect to Warrant

Say that Sam's belief that *p* is *properly basic with respect to warrant* if and only if Sam accepts *p* in the basic way, and furthermore *p* has *warrant* for Sam, accepted in that way. Perceptual beliefs are properly basic in this sense: such beliefs are typically accepted in the basic way, and they often have warrant when accepted in that way. (They are often produced by cognitive faculties functioning properly in a congenial epistemic environment according to a design plan successfully aimed at truth.) The same goes for memory beliefs. Of course, sometimes beliefs are accepted in the basic way but do not have warrant. As we saw earlier, this can be due to cognitive malfunction, or to a cognitive faculty's being impeded by such conditions as rage, lust, ambition, grief, and the like; it can also be because the bit of the design plan governing the production of the belief is aimed not at truth but something else (survival, for example, or self-esteem).

We saw earlier that belief in God in the basic way can be *justified;* one can believe in this basic way without flouting any epistemic duties or obligations. We could put it by saying that *theistic belief can be properly basic with respect to justification.* According to the A/C model I am presenting, theistic belief produced by the *sensus divinitatis* can also be properly basic with respect to *warrant.* It isn't just that the believer in God is within her epistemic rights in accepting theistic belief in the basic way. That is indeed so; more than this, however, this belief can have warrant for the person in question, warrant which is often sufficient for knowledge.

The *sensus divinitatis* is a belief-producing faculty (or power, or mechanism) that under the right conditions produces belief that isn't evidentially based on other beliefs. On this model, our cognitive faculties have been designed and created by God; the design plan, therefore, is a design plan in the literal and paradigmatic sense. It is a blueprint or plan for our ways of cognitive functioning, and it has been developed and instituted by a conscious, intelligent agent. The purpose of the *sensus divinitatis* is to

36

enable us to have true beliefs about God; and when it functions properly, it ordinarily *does* produce true beliefs about God. These beliefs therefore can meet the conditions for warrant; when they do, if they are strong enough, then they constitute knowledge.

Finally, according to the A/C model this natural knowledge of God has in many or most cases been compromised, weakened, reduced, smothered, overlaid, or impeded by sin and its consequences. Due to sin, the knowledge of God provided by the *sensus divinitatis,* prior to faith and regeneration, is both narrowed in scope and partially suppressed. The faculty itself may be *diseased* and thus partly or wholly disabled. There is such a thing as cognitive disease; there is blindness, deafness, inability to tell right from wrong, insanity; and there are analogues of these conditions with respect to the operation of the *sensus divinitatis.* According to Marx and Marxists, as we saw, it is belief in God that is a result of cognitive disease, of dysfunction. From their perspective, belief in God is irrational; there is a failure of rational faculties to work as they should. But here the A/C model stands Freud and Marx on their heads;[8] according to the model, it is really the *unbeliever* who displays epistemic malfunction; failing to believe in God is a result of some kind of dysfunction of the *sensus divinitatis.*

Is Belief in God Warrant-Basic?

If False, Probably Not

As we saw above, Freud doesn't really *argue* that theistic belief has no warrant if taken in the basic way: he seems to assume that such belief is false, and then infers in rather quick and casual fashion that it is produced by wish-fulfillment and hence doesn't have warrant. Here (despite the appearance of carelessness) perhaps Freud's instincts are right: I shall argue that if theistic belief is false, and taken in the basic way, then it probably has no warrant. Why think so? First, note that a false belief can sometimes have a degree of warrant — ordinarily, in a case where the faculty in question is working at the limits of its capability. You see a mountain goat on a distant crag and mistakenly think you see that it has horns; as a matter of fact it is just too far away for you to see clearly, and the truth is it doesn't

---

8. More accurately, what we see here is part of Freud and Marx's extensive borrowing from Christian and Jewish ways of thinking.

have horns. Your belief is false, but has a certain degree of warrant. You are a particle physicist and mistakenly believe that a certain subatomic model is close to the truth: working as you are at the outer limits of the cognitive domain for which our faculties are designed, again, your belief is false but not without warrant.

There is another and more important consideration; we can approach it indirectly as follows. A belief has warrant only if the cognitive process that produces it is *successfully* aimed at the truth — that is, only if there is a high probability that a belief produced by this process is true (given that the process is functioning properly in the sort of epistemic environment for which it is designed). Now a belief can be false, even if it is produced by a process or faculty successfully aimed at truth. It could be that on a given occasion an instrument issues a false reading even though there is a substantial probability that any reading it produces will be true. Consider that a reliable barometer may give a false reading, due to an unusual and improbable confluence of circumstances. (There is a large and sudden drop in the air pressure; the barometer, however, still registers 29.72, because there hasn't been enough time for it to react to the change.)

Similarly for a cognitive process: there might in fact be a high probability that a belief it produces is true (the cognitive process that produces it is *successfully aimed at the truth*), despite the fact that on a given occasion it issues a false belief. (It's reliable, but not infallible.) Couldn't something similar hold for the processes that produce belief in God? Might it not be that belief in God is produced by cognitive processes successfully aimed at the truth, even if that belief is as a matter of fact false? That is, could belief in God be a warranted false belief?

I think not. Say that a *possible world* is a way things could have been. For example, there is a possible world in which Cleveland is larger than New York, and another in which the earth doesn't exist. The *actual world,* of course, is one of the possible worlds: it is the one that actually holds. Some of the possible worlds are more similar to the actual world than others: for example a world in which the earth doesn't exist is less similar, so far forth, than one in which you are a couple of inches taller or shorter than you are in fact, and everything else is as it is in the actual world. We could think of the worlds more similar to the actual world than others as *closer to* the actual world than those others.[9]

9. For a much fuller account of possible worlds see my *The Nature of Necessity* (Oxford: Clarendon, 1984), chap. 4.

Now a proposition is *probable*, with respect to some condition, only if that proposition is true in most of the nearby possible worlds (the worlds similar to the actual world) in which that condition holds. So consider the process that produces theistic belief: if it is successfully aimed at truth, then in most of the nearby possible worlds it produces a true belief. But then it follows that in most of the nearby possible worlds there is such a person as God.

However, that can't be, if the fact is there is no such person as God. For if in fact (in the actual world) there is no such person as God, then a world in which there *is* such a person — an omniscient, omnipotent, wholly good person who has created the world — would be enormously, unimaginably different from the actual world, and enormously dissimilar from it. So if there is no such person as God, it is probably not the case that the process that produces theistic belief, produces a true belief in most of the nearby possible worlds. Therefore, if there is no such person as God, it is unlikely that belief in God is produced by a process that is functioning properly in a congenial epistemic environment according to a design plan successfully aimed at the production of true belief. So if theistic belief is false, it probably has no warrant.

If True, Probably So

On the other hand, if theistic belief is *true,* then it seems likely that it *does* have warrant. For if it is true, then there is indeed such a person as God, a person who has created us in his image (so that we resemble him, among other things, in having the capacity for knowledge), who loves us, who desires that we know and love him, and who is such that it is our end and good to know and love him. But if these things are so, then God would of course intend that we be able to be aware of his presence, and to know something about him. And if that is so, the natural thing to think is that he created us in such a way that we would come to hold such true beliefs as that he is our creator, that we owe him obedience and worship, that he is worthy of worship, that he loves us, and so on. And if *that* is so, then, further, the natural thing to think is that the cognitive processes that *do* produce belief in God are aimed by their designer (God) at producing that belief. But then the belief in question will be produced by cognitive faculties functioning properly according to a design plan successfully aimed at truth: it will therefore have warrant.

This isn't certain; the argument is not deductively valid. It is abstractly possible, I suppose, that God has created us with a faculty for knowing him; for one reason or another, this faculty always malfunctions, and some other faculty created to produce some *other* beliefs often malfunctions in such a way that *it* produces belief in God. Then our belief in God wouldn't have warrant, despite the fact that it is true. This is an abstract possibility, but not much more; it certainly seems unlikely. The more probable thing, at least so far as I can see, is that if in fact theism is true, then theistic belief has warrant. The conclusion to draw, I think, is that the probability of theistic belief's being warranted, given that theism is true, is high.

The *De Jure* Question Is Not Independent of the *De Facto* Question

And here we see the metaphysical or ultimately religious roots of the question concerning the rationality or warrant or lack thereof for belief in God. What you properly take to be rational or warranted depends upon what sort of metaphysical and religious stance you adopt. It depends upon what kind of beings you think human beings are, what sorts of beliefs you think their faculties will produce when they are functioning properly, and which of their faculties or cognitive mechanisms are aimed at the truth. Your view as to what sort of creature a human being is will determine or at any rate heavily influence your views as to whether theistic belief is warranted or not warranted, rational or irrational for human beings. And so the dispute as to whether theistic belief is rational (warranted) can't be settled just by attending to epistemological considerations; it is at bottom not merely an epistemological dispute, but a metaphysical or theological dispute.

You may think humankind is created by God in the image of God — and created both with a natural tendency to see God's hand in the world about us, and with a natural tendency to recognize that we have indeed been created and are beholden to our creator, owing him worship and allegiance. Then, of course, you will not think of belief in God as a manifestation of any kind of intellectual defect. Nor will you think it is a manifestation of a belief-producing power or mechanism that is not aimed at the truth. It is instead a cognitive mechanism whereby we are put in touch with part of reality — indeed by far the most important part of reality. It is in this regard like a deliverance of sense perception, or memory, or reason.

On the other hand, you may think we human beings are the product of blind evolutionary forces; you may think there is no God, and that we are part of a Godless universe. Then you will be inclined to accept the sort of view according to which belief in God is an illusion of some sort, properly traced to wishful thinking or some other cognitive mechanism not aimed at the truth (Freud) or to a sort of disease or dysfunction on the part of the individual or society (Marx).

This dependence of the question of warrant or rationality on the truth or falsehood of theism leads to a very interesting conclusion. If the *warrant* enjoyed by belief in God is related in this way to the *truth* of that belief, then the question whether theistic belief has *warrant* is not after all independent of the question whether theistic belief is *true*. So the *de jure* question we have finally found is not, after all, really independent of the *de facto* question; to answer the former we must answer the latter.

This is important: what it shows is that a successful atheological objection (i.e., an objection to theistic belief) will have to be to the *truth* of theism, not merely to its rationality, or justification, or intellectual respectability, or rational justification, or whatever. The atheologian who wishes to attack theistic belief will have to restrict herself to objections like the argument from evil, or the claim that theism is incoherent, or the idea that in some other way there is strong evidence against theistic belief. She can't any longer adopt the following stance: "Well, I certainly don't know whether theistic belief is *true* — who could know a thing like that? — but I do know this: it is irrational, or unjustified, or not rationally justified, or contrary to reason or intellectually irresponsible or. . . ." There isn't a sensible *de jure* question or criticism that is independent of the *de facto* question.

This fact by itself invalidates an enormous amount of recent and contemporary atheology; for much of that atheology is devoted to *de jure* complaints that are allegedly independent of the *de facto* question. If my argument so far is right, though, there *aren't* any sensible complaints of that sort. (More modestly, none have been so far proposed; it is always possible, I suppose, that someone will come up with one.)

The F&M Complaint Revisited

As we saw in the last chapter, Marx's complaint about religion is that it is produced by cognitive faculties that are malfunctioning; this cognitive dysfunction is due to *social* dysfunction and dislocation. Besides that famous "Religion is the opium of the people" passage, however, Marx doesn't have a lot to say about religious belief — except, of course, for a number of semi-journalistic gibes and japes and other expressions of hostility.[10] I shall therefore concentrate upon Freud, who holds (as we saw in the last chapter) not that theistic belief originates in cognitive malfunction, but that it is an *illusion,* in his technical sense. It finds its origin in *wish-fulfillment,* which, while it is a cognitive process with an important role to play in the total economy of our intellectual life, is nevertheless not aimed at the production of true beliefs. On Freud's view, then, theistic belief, given that it is produced by wish-fulfillment, does not have warrant; it fails to satisfy the condition of being produced by cognitive faculties whose purpose it is to produce true belief. He goes on to characterize religious belief as "neurosis," "illusion," "poison," "intoxicant," and "childishness to be overcome," all on one page of *The Future of an Illusion.*[11]

It is important to see the following point, however. Freud's complaint is that religious belief lacks warrant because it is produced by wishful thinking, which is a cognitive process that is not aimed at the production of true belief; in Freud's words, it is not reality oriented. But even if it were established that wish-fulfillment *is* the source of theistic belief, however, that wouldn't be enough to establish that the latter has no warrant. It must also be established that wish-fulfillment *in this particular manifestation* is not aimed at true belief. The cognitive design plan of human beings is subtle and complex; a source of belief might be such that *in general* it isn't aimed at the formation of true belief, but in some special cases it is. So perhaps this is true of wish-fulfillment; in general its purpose is not that of producing true belief, but in this special case precisely that *is* its purpose. Perhaps human beings have been created by God with a deep need to believe in his presence and goodness and love. Perhaps God has designed us that way in order that we come to believe in him and be aware of his

10. See Karl Marx and Friedrich Engels, *On Religion,* ed. Reinhold Niebuhr (Chico, CA: Scholars Press, 1964). (This is a collection of bits of various writings on religion by Marx and Engels.)

11. *The Future of an Illusion,* trans. and ed. James Strachey (New York and London: Norton, 1961), p. 88. Not to be outdone, a substantial number of subsequent psychologists, sociologists, and anthropologists have followed his lead. Sometimes these suggestions take uncommonly bizarre forms, worthy, almost, to be compared with Freud's own highly imaginative stories about the origin of religion (see above, pp. 21-24). According to Michael P. Carroll, for example, praying the rosary is "a disguised gratification of repressed anal-erotic desires" — a substitute for "playing with one's feces" ("Praying the Rosary: The Anal-erotic Origins of a Popular Catholic Devotion," *Journal for the Scientific Study of Religion* 26, no. 4 [Dec. 1987]: 491).

presence; perhaps this is how God has arranged for us to come to know him. If so, then the particular bit of the cognitive design plan governing the formation of theistic belief is indeed aimed at true belief, even if the belief in question arises from wish-fulfillment. Perhaps God has designed us to know that he is present and loves us by way of creating us with a strong desire for him, a desire that leads to the belief that in fact he is there. Nor is this a mere speculative possibility; something like it is embraced by both St. Augustine ("Our hearts are restless till they rest in thee, O God") and Jonathan Edwards.

And how would Freud or a follower establish that in fact the mechanism whereby human beings come to believe in God (come to believe that there is such a person as God) is *not* in fact aimed at the truth? This is really the crux of the matter. Freud offers no arguments or reasons here at all. As far as I can see, he simply takes it for granted that there is no God and theistic belief is false; he then casts about for some kind of explanation of this widespread phenomenon of mistaken belief. He hits on wish-fulfillment and apparently assumes it is obvious that this mechanism is not "reality oriented," i.e., is not aimed at the production of true belief, and hence lacks warrant. As we have seen, this is a safe assumption if in fact theism *is* false. But then Freud's version of the *de jure* criticism really depends upon his atheism: it isn't an independent criticism at all, and it won't (or shouldn't) have any force for anyone who doesn't share that atheism.

One who believes in God, naturally enough, Christian or Jew or Muslim, is unlikely to acquiesce in the F&M claim that belief in God has no warrant. (It is only a certain variety of 'liberal' theologian, crazed by thirst for novelty and the desire to accommodate current secularity, who might agree with F&M here.) Indeed, she will see the shoe as on the other foot. According to St. Paul, it is *unbelief* that is a result of dysfunction, or brokenness, failure to function properly, or impedance of rational faculties. Unbelief, he says, is a result of sin; it originates in an effort, as Romans 1 puts it, to "suppress the truth in unrighteousness."[12] Indeed, unbelief can

---

12. Of course it isn't Paul's idea that those who don't believe are by that very fact seen to be more sinful than those who do. On the contrary: just a couple of chapters later he says we are *all* involved in sin, including, of course, *himself* ("Wretched man that I am! Who will rescue me from this body of death?"). Furthermore, the malfunction that lies at the root of unbelief is not necessarily that of the unbeliever herself. Some kinds of unbelief (see below, p. 49) are like blindness; upon seeing a blind man, the disciples asked Jesus, "Rabbi, who sinned, this man or his parents, that he was born blind?" (John 9:2) — to which Jesus replied that this blindness was due neither to the man's own sin nor that of his parents.

also be seen as resulting from wish-fulfillment — a result of the desire to live in a world without God, a world in which there is no one to whom I owe worship and obedience.

What we have seen so far, therefore, is that, despite the complaints of Marx and Freud and their allies, belief in God can perfectly well be justified and have warrant. In the next chapter I'll extend the A/C model to cover belief in the whole panoply of Christian belief.

CHAPTER FOUR

The Extended A/C Model

According to the Aquinas/Calvin (A/C) model, theistic belief (belief in God) has warrant, indeed, sufficient warrant for knowledge. The central feature of this model is the stipulation that God has created us human beings with a belief-producing process or source of belief, the *sensus divinitatis;* this source works under various conditions to produce beliefs about God, including, of course, beliefs that immediately entail his existence. Belief produced in this way, I said, can easily meet the conditions for warrant.

So far, therefore, we have been thinking just about belief that there is such a person as God. But of course specifically Christian belief goes well beyond belief in God; it includes first, the ideas that human beings have fallen into sin and rebelled against God, and second, the incomparable divine response: God sent his Son into the world, and through his life, sacrificial death, and resurrection we human beings can once more be in a right relationship with God. My aim is to extend the A/C model so that it applies to full-blooded Christian belief in sin, atonement, and salvation. I hope to show how it can be that Christians can be justified, rational, and warranted in holding full-blooded Christian belief — and not just 'ignorant fundamentalists', but sophisticated, aware, educated, twenty-first-century people who have read their Freud and Nietzsche, their Hume and Mackie (their Dennett and Dawkins). Justification is easy enough: just as for theistic belief, I'll argue that many or most Christians not only *can* be but also *are* justified in holding their characteristic beliefs.

According to this extended A/C model, specifically Christian belief can have warrant and thus constitute knowledge. The model will include the main lines of ecumenical classic Christian belief. It also needs a certain amount of additional detail; this additional detail is broadly Reformed or

Calvinist in inspiration, but I shall develop it in my own way. I shall use the model to argue three things. First, I will use it to argue that Christian belief *can* very well be warranted; there is a perfectly viable epistemological account of how it is that it should have this virtue, and no cogent objections to its having it. Second, I'll argue (as I did with respect to theistic belief) that if Christian belief is *true,* then it probably *is* both rational and warranted for most Christians. Thus I'll be attacking again that stance I mentioned above — the claim that of course we don't know whether Christian belief is, in fact, true (that's a pretty tall order, after all), but we do know that even if it happens to be true, it isn't rational or warranted. Third, I'll recommend the story or model I present as a good way, though not necessarily the only good way, for Christians to think about the epistemological status of Christian belief.

Now our question is whether these beliefs are justified, rational, and warranted. But justification is easily dealt with. First, justification, taken in terms of intellectual rights and obligations, is no more problematic here than in the case of theism. Clearly, a person (including a highly educated, wholly with-it, twenty-first-century person who has read all the latest objections to Christian belief) *could* be justified in accepting these and other Christian beliefs and *would* be so justified if (for example) after careful and nonculpable reflection and investigation into the alleged objections and defeaters, she still found those beliefs wholly compelling. She could hardly be blamed for believing what strongly seems, after extensive investigation, to be the truth of the matter. (She's supposed to believe what seems *false* to her?)

These observations, however, won't or shouldn't quiet the critics. For even if Christian believers are *justified* in their beliefs, they might still be *irrational* and thus wholly without warrant. After all, even the beliefs of a madman or of a victim of a Cartesian evil demon can be justified. Well, then, what about rationality and warrant? A belief is rational if it is produced by cognitive faculties that are functioning properly and successfully aimed at truth (i.e., aimed at the production of true belief) — as opposed, for example, to being the product of wishful thinking or cognitive malfunction. Now warrant, the property enough of which distinguishes knowledge from mere true belief, is a property or quantity had by a belief if and only if (so I say) that belief is produced by cognitive faculties functioning properly in a congenial epistemic environment according to a design plan successfully aimed at truth. Because rationality (in the sense of proper function of rational powers) is included in warrant, the real question, here, is whether Christian belief does or can have warrant.

Initial Statement of the Model

According to the extended A/C model, Christian belief does indeed have warrant. In essence, the model goes like this. First, God has created us human beings *in his own image.* This centrally involves our resembling God in being *persons* — that is, beings with *intellect* and *will.* Like God, we are the sort of beings who have beliefs and understanding: we have intellect. There is also will, however: we also resemble God in having affections (loves and hates), in forming aims and intentions, and in being able to act to accomplish these aims and intentions. Call this the *broad* image of God.

But human beings as originally created also displayed a *narrow* image: they had extensive and intimate knowledge of God, and the right affections, including gratitude for God's goodness. They loved and hated what was lovable and hateful; above all, they knew and loved God.

Part of the broad image was the *sensus divinitatis.* Now the extended A/C model retains this feature and adds more. First, it adds that we human beings have fallen into sin, a calamitous condition from which we require salvation — a salvation we are unable to accomplish by our own efforts. This sin alienates us from God and makes us unfit for communion with him. Our fall into sin has had cataclysmic consequences, both affective and cognitive. As to affective consequences, our affections — our loves and hates — are skewed, and our hearts now harbor deep and radical evil: we don't love God above all; instead, we love ourselves above all. In this way the narrow image was nearly destroyed.

There were also ruinous *cognitive* consequences. Our original knowledge of God and of his marvelous beauty, glory, and loveliness has been severely compromised; in this way the broad image was damaged, distorted. In particular, the *sensus divinitatis* has been damaged and deformed; because of our fall into sin, we no longer know God in the same natural and unproblematic way in which we know each other and the world around us. Still further, sin induces in us a *resistance* to the deliverances of the *sensus divinitatis,* muted as they are by the first factor; we don't *want* to pay attention to its deliverances.

We are unable by our own efforts to extricate ourselves from this quagmire; God himself, however, has provided a remedy for sin and its ruinous effects, a means of salvation from sin and restoration to his favor and fellowship. This remedy is made available in the life, atoning suffering and death, and resurrection of his divine Son, Jesus Christ. Salvation involves, among other things, rebirth and regeneration, a process (beginning in the present life and reaching fruition in the next) that involves a restoration and repair of the image of God in us.

So far, what we have here is the "mere Christianity" of which C. S. Lewis spoke;[1] we now come to a more specifically cognitive side of the model. God needed a way to inform human beings of many times and places of the scheme of salvation he has graciously made available. No doubt he could have done this in a thousand different ways; in fact, according to the model, he chose to do so in the following way. First, there were the prophets and the apostles, and the Bible, a collection of writings by human authors, but specially inspired by God in such a way that he can be said to be its principal author. Second, he has sent the Holy Spirit, promised by Christ before his death and resurrection.[2] And third, a principal work of the Holy Spirit with respect to us human beings is the production in us human beings of the gift of *faith,* that "firm and certain knowledge of God's benevolence towards us, founded upon the truth of the freely given promise in Christ, both revealed to our minds and sealed upon our hearts through the Holy Spirit" of which Calvin speaks.[3] By virtue of the internal testimony or witness of the Holy Spirit, we come to see the truth of the central Christian affirmations.

Sin and Its Nature

Now that we have the extended model before us in outline, we must take a more detailed look into a couple of its various aspects, starting with the nature of sin and its consequences.

What is sin? Whatever it is, it is both astonishingly deep and deeply elusive. According to the model, there is first the phenomenon of *sinning:* of doing what is wrong, what is contrary to God's will. This is something for which the sinner is *responsible;* he is guilty and deserves blame — but only if he recognizes that what he does *is* sin, or is culpable in failing to recognize that it is. There is also the condition of *being in* sin, a state in which

1. *Mere Christianity* (New York: Macmillan, 1958).

2. See, e.g., John 14:25-26: "All this have I spoken while still with you. But the Counselor, the Holy Spirit, whom the Father will send in my name, will teach you all things and will remind you of everything I have said to you."

3. John Calvin, *Institutes of the Christian Religion,* ed. John T. McNeill and trans. Ford Lewis Battles (Philadelphia: Westminster, 1960 [1559]), III.ii.7, p. 551. References to the *Institutes* are to this edition.

we human beings find ourselves from our very birth. A traditional Christian term for this condition is 'original sin'. Unlike a sinful act I perform, original sin need not be thought of as something for which I am culpable (original *sin* is not necessarily original *guilt*); insofar as I am born in this predicament, my being in it is not within my control and not up to me. (In any event there is plenty of opportunity for culpability with respect to the less original variety of sin.)

How does it happen that we human beings are mired in this desperate and deplorable condition? The traditional Christian answer: it is as a result of the sinful actions of Adam and Eve, our original parents and the first human beings. Whether this is indeed how it happened is a matter on which the model need not take a stand; what *is* part of the model is that in fact we are in the condition. G. K. Chesterton once remarked that of all the doctrines of Christianity, the doctrine of original sin has the strongest claim to "empirical verifiability" (the quality that back in the palmy days of positivism was widely trumpeted as the very criterion of "cognitive meaningfulness"); it has been abundantly verified in the wars, cruelty, and general hatefulness that have characterized human history from its very inception to the present. Indeed, no century has seen more organized hatred, contempt, and cruelty than the late and unlamented twentieth; and none has seen it on as grand a scale.

There is a deep and obvious *social* side of sin. We human beings are deeply communal; we learn from parents, teachers, peers, and others, both by imitation and by precept. We acquire beliefs in this way, but just as important (and perhaps less self-consciously), we acquire attitudes and affections, loves and hates. Because of our social nature, sin and its effects can be like a contagion that spreads from one to another, eventually corrupting an entire society or segment of it.

Original sin involves both intellect and will; it is both cognitive and affective. It is both a matter of knowledge, and also of loves and hates. On the one hand, it carries with it a sort of *blindness,* a sort of imperceptiveness, dullness, stupidity. This is a cognitive limitation that first of all prevents its victim from proper knowledge of God and his beauty, glory, and love; it also prevents him from seeing what is worth loving and what worth hating, what should be sought and what rejected. It therefore compromises both knowledge of fact and knowledge of value.

But sin is also and perhaps primarily an *affective* disorder or malfunction. Our affections are skewed, directed to the wrong objects; we love and hate the wrong things. Instead of seeking first the kingdom of God,

I am inclined to seek first my own personal aggrandizement, bending all my efforts toward making myself look good. Instead of loving God above all and my neighbor as myself, I am inclined to love myself above all and, indeed, often inclined to resent or even hate God and my neighbor.

Much of this hostility springs from *pride*, that aboriginal sin, and from consequent attempts at self-aggrandizement. We think of getting the world's good things as a zero-sum game: any bit of it you have is a bit I can't have — and want. If I am an academic, I want to be better known than you, so when you do something noteworthy I feel a prick of envy. I may want to be rich. What counts is not how much money I have, absolutely speaking; what counts is whether I have more than you, or most people, or everybody else. But then you and others are obstacles to the fulfillment of my desires; I can thus come to resent and hate you.

And God himself, the source of my very being, can also be a threat. In my prideful desire for autonomy and self-sufficiency I can come to resent the presence of someone upon whom I depend for my every breath and by comparison with whom I am small potatoes indeed. I can therefore come to hate him too. I want to be autonomous, beholden to no one. Perhaps this is the deepest root of the condition of sin, and a motivation for atheism as wish-fulfillment.[4]

The defect here is affective, not intellectual. Our affections are disordered; they no longer work according to God's original design plan for human beings. There is a failure of proper function, an affective disorder, a sort of madness of the will. In this condition, we know (in some way and to some degree) what is to be loved (what is objectively lovable), but we nevertheless perversely turn away from what ought to be loved and instead love something else. (As the popular song has it: "My heart has a mind of its own.") We know (at some level) what is right, but find ourselves drawn to what is wrong; we know that we should love God and our neighbor, but we nonetheless prefer not to.

Of course, this raises an ancient question, one going back to Socrates: Can a person really do what she knows or believes is wrong? If she sees what is right, how can she still do what is wrong? The answer is simple

---

4. This desire for autonomy, self-definition, and self-creation can assume quite remarkable proportions: according to Richard Rorty, the famous philosopher Martin Heidegger felt guilty about living in a world he hadn't himself created (now there's a tender conscience!), refused to feel at home in any such world, and couldn't stand the thought that he was not his own creation (*Contingency, Irony, and Solidarity* [Cambridge: Cambridge University Press, 1989], p. 109).

enough: she *sees* what is right, but *prefers* what is wrong. Socrates fails to see the possibility of *affective* disorder, as opposed to intellectual deficiency or ignorance. In the *absence* of affective disorder, perhaps, indeed, I cannot see the good but prefer the evil, knowing that it is evil. Unfortunately, however, we can't count on the absence of that disorder; sin is, in large part, precisely such disorder. Because of this affective malfunction, I desire and seek what I know or believe is bad.

As both Augustine and Pascal noted, this whole complex and confusing collection of attitudes, affections, and beliefs that constitute the state of sin is a fertile field for ambiguity and self-deception.[5] According to the extended A/C model, we human beings typically have at least some knowledge of God, and some grasp of what is required of us; this is so even in the state of sin and even apart from regeneration. The condition of sin involves *damage* to the *sensus divinitatis,* but not obliteration; it remains partially functional in most of us. We therefore typically have some grasp of God's presence and properties and demands, but this knowledge is covered over, impeded, suppressed. We are prone to hate God but, confusingly, in some way also inclined to love and seek him; we are prone to hate our neighbor, to see her as a competitor for scarce goods, but also, paradoxically, to prize her and love her.

Perhaps I recognize, in a sort of semi-subliminal way, that there is deep disorder and worse in my life. I half-recognize the selfishness and self-centeredness that characterizes most of my waking moments. Perhaps I note that even (or perhaps especially) in private soliloquy, where there is no question of influencing others, I imaginatively create, rehearse, and contemplate various situations in which I come out victorious, or heroic, or virtuously long-suffering, or anyway abundantly admirable. Perhaps I also glimpse the foolishness and corruption here, but most of the time I pay no attention. I ignore it; I hide it from myself, escaping into work, projects, family, the whole realm of the everyday. (As Pascal says, "Right now I can't be bothered; I have to return my opponent's serve."[6])

This ambiguity extends even deeper. One can't help but concur with the apostle Paul: "For what I do is not the good I want to do; no, the evil I do not want to do — this I keep on doing" (Rom. 7:19). I often do what

---

5. For contemporary comment, see Bas van Fraassen's "The Peculiar Effects of Love and Desire," in *Perspectives on Self-Deception,* ed. A. Rorty and B. McLaughlin (Berkeley: University of California Press, 1988). Van Fraassen offers a subtle account of some of the tangled depths of self-deception.

6. Quoted in van Fraassen, "Peculiar Effects."

I recognize is the wrong thing, even though I don't *want* to do the wrong thing; and I don't do what's right, even though I do want to do what's right. It seems that I don't do what I want to do and, instead, do what I don't want to. Or is it instead that when I do wrong, I want to do that very thing, but don't then think it *is* wrong (though at other times — later, maybe — I see perfectly well that it is, and very much wish that I hadn't done it)? Or is it rather that at that time I *do* see (to at least some degree) that it's wrong, or *would* clearly see that it is if I paid attention (and I also semi-know *that* fact then), but I *don't* pay attention, because I want to do this thing? Or is it that when I do something wrong, *then* I *do* want to do that wrong thing, knowing (in a sort of muffled way) that it *is* wrong, even though I don't want to *want* to do the wrong thing? Or is it that when I am wanting to do what is wrong, I don't even raise for myself the question whether it is wrong? Who can tell?

Revealed to Our Minds

The point of the extended A/C model, of course, is to show how specifically Christian belief — belief, not just in God, but in Trinity, incarnation, Christ's resurrection, atonement, forgiveness of sins, salvation, regeneration, eternal life — can be both reasonable and warranted. How can we think of these beliefs — some of which, as the philosopher David Hume loved to point out, go entirely contrary to ordinary human experience — as reasonable or rational, let alone warranted? The materials for an answer lie close at hand. Actually, the materials have lain close at hand for several centuries — certainly since the publication of Jonathan Edwards's *Religious Affections*[7] and John Calvin's *Institutes of the Christian Religion*. As a matter of fact, they have lain close at hand for much longer than that: much of what Calvin says can be usefully seen as development of remarks of Thomas Aquinas and Bonaventure. Indeed, these materials go much further back yet, all the way back to the New Testament, in particular the gospel of John and the epistles of Paul.

My development of these materials — the extended A/C model — will show how *Christian* belief can be both rational and warranted — not just for 'ignorant fundamentalists' or benighted medievals but for informed

---

7. Ed. John Smith (New Haven: Yale University Press, 1959 [1746]). Page references to *Religious Affections* throughout are to this edition.

and educated twenty-first-century Christians who are entirely aware of all the artillery that has been rolled out against Christian belief since the Enlightenment. For the sake of definiteness I shall be following one particular and traditional way of thinking about our knowledge of Christian truth. I believe that this account or something similar is in fact rather close to the sober truth, but other models fitting other traditions can easily be constructed. My extended model will have one further feature: it will complete and deepen the previous account of our knowledge of God. The central themes of this extended model are the Bible, the internal testimony of the Holy Spirit, and faith.

According to the model (as we've seen), we human beings were created in the image of God. Sadly enough, we fell into sin, a ruinous condition from which we require rescue and redemption. God proposed and instituted a plan of salvation: the life, atoning suffering and death, and resurrection of Jesus Christ, the incarnate second person of the Trinity. The result for us is the possibility of salvation from sin, renewed relationship with God, and eternal life. But (and here we come to the specifically epistemological extension of the model) God needed a way in which to inform us — us human beings of many different times and places — of the scheme of salvation he has graciously made available.[8] He chose to do so by way of a three-tiered cognitive process. First, he spoke through the prophets and apostles and arranged for the production of *Scripture,* the *Bible,* a library of books or writings each of which has a human author, but of which God himself is its principal author. In this library he proposes much for our belief and action, but there is a central theme and focus (and for this reason this collection of books is itself a book): the gospel, the good news of the way of salvation God has graciously offered.[9] Correlative with Scripture and necessary to its properly serving its purpose is the

8. It is no part of the model to suggest that explicit beliefs about Jesus Christ are a necessary condition of salvation: the Old Testament patriarchs, for example, are counted as heroes of faith in the New Testament (Hebrews 11) despite the fact that they presumably had no explicit beliefs about Jesus Christ. They trusted God to do whatever was necessary for their salvation and shalom; but they had no particular idea as to just what that might be. Furthermore, it is no part of the model to assert that all who believe these things, come to believe them by way of the processes proposed in the model: perhaps, for example, the apostles came to believe these truths in quite a different fashion.

9. But hasn't the historical critical Scripture scholarship of the last two hundred years cast grave doubt on the reliability of the Bible and the claim that it is specially inspired by God? This suggestion is a proposed *defeater* for Christian belief; see below, Chapter Eight.

second element of this three-tiered cognitive process: the presence and action of the Holy Spirit promised by Christ himself before his death and resurrection,[10] and invoked and celebrated in the epistles of the apostle Paul.[11] By virtue of the work of the Holy Spirit in the hearts of those to whom faith is given, the ravages of sin (including the cognitive damage) are repaired, gradually or suddenly, to a greater or lesser extent. Furthermore, it is by virtue of the activity of the Holy Spirit that Christians come to grasp, endorse, and rejoice in the truth of the great things of the gospel. It is thus by virtue of this activity that the Christian believes that "God was reconciling the world to himself in Christ, not counting men's sins against them" (2 Cor. 5:19).

According to John Calvin, the principal work of the Holy Spirit is the production (in the hearts of Christian believers) of the third element of the process, *faith.* Like the regeneration of which it is a part, faith is a gift; it is given to anyone who is willing to accept it. Faith, says Calvin, is "a firm and certain knowledge of God's benevolence towards us, founded upon the truth of the freely given promise in Christ, both revealed to our minds and sealed upon our hearts through the Holy Spirit."[12] Faith therefore involves an explicitly cognitive element; it is, says Calvin, *knowledge* — knowledge of the availability of redemption and salvation through the person and work of Jesus Christ — and it is revealed to our minds. To have faith, therefore, is to know and hence *believe* something or other. But (as we shall see in more detail in Chapter Six) faith also involves the *affections:* it is "sealed upon our hearts." By virtue of this sealing, the believer not only knows about the scheme of salvation God has prepared (according to James 2:19 the devils also know about that, and they shudder); she is also heartily grateful to the Lord for it, and loves him on this account; she accepts the proffered gift and commits herself to living a life of gratitude.[13]

10. E.g., John 14:26: "but the Counselor, the Holy Spirit, whom the Father will send in my name, will teach you all things and will remind you of everything I have said to you." See also John 14:11: "Believe me when I say that I am in the Father and the Father is in me," and 15:26: "When the Counselor comes, whom I will send to you from the Father, the Spirit of truth who goes out from the Father, he will testify about me."

11. E.g., Eph. 1:17: "I keep asking that the God of our Lord Jesus Christ, the glorious Father, may give you the spirit of wisdom and revelation, so that you may know him better." And 1 Cor. 2:12-13: "We have not received the spirit of the world, but the Spirit who is from God, that we may understand what God has freely given us. This is what we speak, not in words taught us by human wisdom but in words taught by the Spirit."

12. *Institutes* III.ii.7, p. 551.

13. Presented in this brief and undeveloped way, this model can seem unduly individ-

But isn't all this just endorsing a wholly outmoded and discredited fundamentalism, that condition than which, according to many secularists, none lesser can be conceived? I fully realize that the dreaded f-word will be trotted out to stigmatize any model of this kind. Before responding, however, we must first look into the use of this term 'fundamentalist'. On the most common contemporary academic use of the term, it is a term of abuse or disapprobation, rather like 'son of a bitch' — more exactly, 'sonofabitch', or, perhaps still more exactly (at least according to those authorities who look to the Old West as normative on matters of pronunciation) 'sumbitch'. When the term is used in this way, no definition of it is ordinarily given. (If you called someone a sumbitch, would you feel obliged first to define the term?) But there is a bit more to the meaning of 'fundamentalist' (in this widely current use): it isn't *simply* a term of abuse. In addition to its emotive force, it does have *some* cognitive content, and ordinarily denotes relatively conservative theological views. That makes it more like '*stupid* sumbitch' than 'sumbitch *simpliciter.* But it isn't exactly like *that* term either, because its cognitive content can expand and contract on demand; its content seems to depend upon who is using it. In the mouths of certain liberal theologians, for example, it tends to denote anyone who accepts traditional Christianity, including Augustine, Aquinas, Luther, Calvin, and Barth; in the mouths of devout secularists like Richard Dawkins or Daniel Dennett, on the other hand, it tends to denote anyone who believes there is such a person as God. The explanation is that the term has a certain indexical element: its cognitive content is given by the phrase "considerably to the right, theologically speaking, of me and my enlightened friends." The full meaning of the term, therefore (in this use) can be given by something like "stupid sumbitch whose theological opinions are considerably to the right of mine."

It is therefore hard to take seriously the charge that the views I'm suggesting are fundamentalist; more exactly, it is hard to take it seriously as a *charge.* For the alleged charge means only that these views are rather more conservative than those of the objector, together with the expression of a certain distaste for the views or those who hold them. But how is *that* an objection to anything, and why should it warrant the contempt and

---

ualistic. But of course it doesn't at all preclude the importance of the Christian community and the church to the belief of the individual Christian. It is the church or community that proclaims the gospel, guides the neophyte into it, and supports, instructs, encourages, and edifies believers of all sorts and conditions.

contumely that goes with the term? An *argument* of some kind against those conservative views would be of interest, but merely pointing out that they differ from the objector's (even with the addition of that abusive emotive force) is not.

But how does this model, with its excursion into theology, serve as a model for a way in which Christian belief has or could have justification, rationality, warrant? The answer is simplicity itself. These beliefs do not come to the Christian just by way of memory, perception, reason, testimony, the *sensus divinitatis,* or any other of the cognitive faculties or processes with which we human beings were originally created; they come instead by way of the work of the Holy Spirit, who gets us to accept, causes us to see the truth of these great truths of the gospel. These beliefs don't come just by way of the normal operation of our natural faculties; they are a supernatural gift. Still, the Christian who has received this gift of faith will of course be *justified* (in the basic sense of the term) in believing as he does; there will be nothing contrary to epistemic or other duty in so believing (and indeed, once he has accepted the gift, it may not be within his power to withhold belief).

Given the model, however, the beliefs in question will typically (or at least often) have the other kinds of epistemic values we have been considering as well. First, they will be rational: there need be no cognitive malfunction in the believer; all of her cognitive faculties can be functioning properly. Second, on the model, these beliefs will also have *warrant* for the believer: they will be produced in her by a belief-producing process[14] that is functioning properly in an appropriate cognitive environment (the one for which they were designed) according to a design plan successfully aimed at the production of true beliefs.

In this chapter I have outlined a model — the extended Aquinas/Calvin model — according to which Christian belief can have warrant. In the next couple of chapters, we'll take a look at a central element of that model, the phenomenon of *faith.*

---

14. Of course *this* belief-producing process isn't exactly like the others — memory, perception, reason, and even the *sensus divinitatis;* that is because these others are all part of our original increated cognitive equipment, while (according to the model) the cognitive process here involves a special, supernatural activity on the part of the Holy Spirit. But this doesn't so much as suggest that its deliverances can't enjoy warrant, and warrant sufficient for knowledge.

CHAPTER FIVE

Faith

Now faith is the substance of things hoped for, the evidence of things not seen.

Hebrews 11:1 KJV

Faith is the great cop-out, the great excuse to evade the need to think and evaluate evidence. Faith is belief in spite of, even perhaps because of, the lack of evidence.

Richard Dawkins[1]

As we saw in the last chapter, an essential element of the A/C model is this idea of *faith*. I'll begin by saying something further about this central part of the extended model. The first thing to note is that the term 'faith', like nearly any philosophically useful term, is used variously, in a number of different but analogically connected senses. According to Mark Twain's Huckleberry Finn, faith is "believing what you know ain't so"; this only slightly exaggerates a common use of the term to denote a belief that lacks warrant, and indeed is unlikely with respect to what does have warrant for the believer.[2] A mother who believes in the teeth of the evidence that her son is in fact still alive will be said to have faith that he is still alive. It is in

---

1. "A Scientist's Case against God," an edited version of Dawkins's speech at the Edinburgh International Science Festival on April 15, 1992, published in *The Independent*, April 20, 1992.
2. As in the above quote from Richard Dawkins.

connection with this use that one thinks of 'a leap of faith', which is rather like a leap in the dark. A second way the term is used is to denote a vague and generalized trust that has no specific object, a confidence that things will go right, a sort of optimistic sitting loose with respect to the future, trusting that one can deal with whatever happens. To have faith in this sense is to "accept the universe," as the nineteenth-century transcendentalist Margaret Fuller was said to have declared she did.[3]

In setting out the model, however, I am using the term in a different sense from any of those. My sense will be much closer to that which the Heidelberg Catechism ascribes to "true faith":

> True faith is not only a knowledge and conviction that everything God reveals in his word is true; it is also a deep-rooted assurance, created in me by the Holy Spirit through the gospel, that, out of sheer grace earned for us by Christ, not only others, but I too, have had my sins forgiven, have been made forever right with God, and have been granted salvation. (A. 21)

We can think of this account as making more explicit the content of the definition of faith offered by Calvin in the *Institutes* (above, p. 48). The first thing to see is that faith, so taken, is an epistemic or *cognitive* state or activity. It isn't *merely* a cognitive activity, because it also involves both the affections and the will. (It is a knowledge which is *sealed to our hearts* as well as revealed to our minds.) But even if faith is *more* than cognitive, it is also and *at least* a cognitive activity. It is a matter of "knowledge," Calvin says, and hence involves *believing* something. The Christian, on this account, doesn't merely find her identity in the Christian story, or live in it or out of it; she *believes* it, takes the story to be the sober truth.

Now what one believes are propositions. To have faith, therefore, is (at least) to believe some propositions. Which ones? Not, for example, that the world is the sort of place in which human beings can flourish, or even or primarily that there is such a person as God. Indeed, on this model it isn't really by *faith* that one knows that there is such a person as God. Faith is instead "a firm and certain knowledge of God's benevolence towards us" (Calvin), a firm and certain knowledge that "not only others, but I too, have had my sins forgiven, have been made forever right with

---

3. To which Carlyle retorted "Gad! She'd better!" Mark Twain, on the other hand, claimed he hadn't heard it had been offered to her.

God, and have been granted salvation" (Heidelberg Catechism A. 21) — i.e., a firm and certain knowledge of God's plan whereby we fallen humans can attain shalom, flourishing, well-being, happiness, felicity, salvation, all of which are essentially a matter of being rightly related to God.[4] So the propositional object of faith is the whole magnificent scheme of salvation God has arranged. To have faith is to know that and how God has made it possible for us human beings to escape the ravages of sin and be restored to a right relationship with him; it is therefore a knowledge of the main lines of the Christian gospel. The content of faith is just the central teachings of the gospel; it is contained in the intersection of the great Christian creeds.

What is at issue, in faith, furthermore, is not just knowing that there *is* such a scheme (as we saw above, the devils believe that, and they shudder), but also and most importantly, that this scheme applies to and is available to *me*. So what I know, in faith, is the main lines of specifically Christian teaching — together, we might say, with its application to myself. Christ died for *my* sins, thus making it possible for *me* to be reconciled with God. Faith is initially and fundamentally *practical;* it is a knowledge of the good news and of its application to me, and of what I must do to receive the benefits it proclaims. Still, faith itself is a matter of belief rather than action, it is believing something rather than doing something.

How Does Faith Work?

The principal answer is that faith is a work — the main work, according to Calvin — of the Holy Spirit; it is produced in us by the Holy Spirit. The suggestion that belief in the central elements of the Christian gospel is a result of some special work of the Holy Spirit is often thought of as especially the teaching of such Calvinist thinkers as Edwards and John Calvin himself. It is indeed central to their teaching, and here the model follows them. But on this point as on so many others, Calvin, despite his pugnacious noise about the pestilential papists and their colossal offenses, may be seen as following out and developing a line of thought already to be found in Thomas Aquinas. "The believer," says Aquinas, "has sufficient motive for believing,

---

4. I take it this is a definition or description of faith by way of presenting a *paradigm* of it: *fully formed* and *well-developed* faith will be like this. Thus a person who (for example) believes these things, but without the firmness sufficient for *knowledge,* can still be said to have faith.

for he is moved by the authority of divine teaching confirmed by miracles and, what is more, *by the inward instigation of the divine invitation.*"[5] Here we have (embryonically, at any rate) that same trio of processes: there is *belief,* there is the *divine teaching* (as given in Scripture) which is the object of that belief, and there is also special divine activity in the production of the belief ("the inward instigation of the divine invitation").[6]

What sort of phenomenology is involved in this epistemic process: what does it seem like from the inside? In the model, the beliefs constituting faith are typically taken as basic; that is, they are not accepted by way of argument from other propositions or on the evidential basis of other propositions[7] in this way, though perhaps some believers do in fact reason this way. But in the model it goes differently.

We read Scripture, or something presenting scriptural teaching, or hear the gospel preached, or are told of it by parents, or encounter a scriptural teaching as the conclusion of an argument (or conceivably even as an object of ridicule), or in some other way encounter a proclamation of the Word. What is said simply seems right; it seems compelling; one finds oneself saying "Yes, that's right, that's the truth of the matter; this is indeed the word of the Lord." I read, "God was in Christ, reconciling the world to himself"; I come to think: "Right, that's true; God really was in Christ,

---

5. *Summa Theologiae* II-II, Q. 2, a. 9, reply obj. 3 (my emphasis). According to Aquinas, therefore, faith is produced in human beings by God's action: "for since in assenting to the things of faith a person is raised above his own nature, he has this assent from a supernatural source influencing him; this source is God. The assent of faith, which is its principal act, therefore, has as its cause God, moving us inwardly through grace." ST II-II, Q. 6, a. 1, resp.

6. According to Aquinas, some of the items proposed by God for our belief can also be the objects of *scientia;* when they are, they are not accepted by faith, for it isn't possible, he thinks, to have both *scientia* and faith with respect to the same proposition. Since *scientia* is often translated as 'knowledge', this makes it look as if Calvin contradicts Aquinas when he says that faith is a sure and certain *knowledge* of God's benevolence towards us. Appearances are deceiving, however, and there is no contradiction here. *Scientia* for Aquinas isn't just any kind of knowledge; it is a very special relation between a person and a proposition; it is one that holds when the person sees that the proposition follows from first principles she sees to be true. Thus *scientia* is a much narrower term than our term 'knowledge'. When Calvin says that faith is a sure and certain knowledge of God's benevolence to us, he isn't ascribing to faith a status Aquinas denies it.

7. Of course, they *could* be accepted on the basis of other propositions, and perhaps in some cases are. A believer could reason as follows: I have strong historical and archeological evidence for the reliability of the Bible (or the Church, or my parents, or some other authority); the Bible teaches the great things of the gospel; so probably these things are true. But to think these things *probably* true falls short of that "conviction" and "deep-rooted assurance."

reconciling the world to himself!" And I may also think something a bit different, something *about* that proposition: that it is indeed a divine teaching or revelation, that, in Calvin's words, it is "from God." What one hears or reads seems clearly and obviously true, and (at any rate in paradigm cases) seems also to be something the Lord is intending to teach. So faith may have the phenomenology that goes with suddenly seeing something to be true: "Right! Now I see that this is indeed true and what the Lord is teaching!" Or perhaps the conviction arises slowly, and only after long and hard study, thought, discussion, prayer. Or perhaps it is a matter of a belief's having been there all along (from childhood, perhaps), but now being transformed, renewed, intensified, made vivid and alive. This process can go on in a thousand ways; but in each case there is presentation or proposal of central Christian teaching, and by way of response, the phenomenon of being convinced, coming to see, forming a conviction. There is the reading or hearing, and then there is the belief or conviction that what one reads or hears is true and a teaching of the Lord.

According to the model, this conviction comes by way of the activity of the Holy Spirit. (Calvin speaks here of the internal "testimony" or "witness" of the Holy Spirit; Aquinas, of the divine "instigation" and "invitation.") On the model, there is both Scripture and the divine activity leading to human belief. God himself (on the model) is the principal author of Scripture; Scripture is most importantly a message, a communication from God to humankind; Scripture is a word from the Lord.[8] But then this just is a special case of the pervasive process of testimony, by which, as a matter of fact, we learn most of what we know. From this point of view Scripture is as much a matter of testimony as is a letter you receive from a friend. What is proposed for our belief in Scripture, therefore, just *is* testimony — divine testimony. So the term "testimony" is appropriate here. On the other hand, there is also the special work of the Holy Spirit in getting us to believe, in enabling us to see the truth

---

8. On this model (*pace* many twentieth-century Christian theologians) it is not the case that revelation occurs just by way of *events,* which must then be properly interpreted. No doubt this does indeed happen; but much of Scripture is centrally a matter of God's speaking, of his telling us things we need to know, of his communicating *propositions* to us. See Nicholas Wolterstorff's *Divine Discourse* (Cambridge: Cambridge University Press, 1995) for a specific account of precisely how it could be that the Bible constitutes divine speech, and a divine communication to us. For the sake of definiteness, in what follows I shall incorporate in the model the proposition that something like Wolterstorff's account is in fact correct. (Of course other accounts could also serve in the model.)

of what is proposed. Here Aquinas's terms "invitation" and "instigation" are more appropriate.

So Scripture is indeed testimony; but it is testimony of a very special kind. First, the principal testifier is God. It also differs from ordinary testimony in that in this case, unlike most others, there is both a principal testifier and subordinate testifiers: the human authors.[9] There is still another difference: it is the instigation of the Holy Spirit, on this model, that gets us to see and believe that the propositions proposed for our beliefs in Scripture really *are* a word from the Lord. This case also differs from the usual run of testimony, then, in that the Holy Spirit not only writes the letter (appropriately inspires the human authors), but also does something special to enable one to believe and appropriate its contents. So this testimony is not the usual run of testimony; it is testimony nonetheless. According to the model, therefore, faith is the belief in the great things of the gospel that results from the internal instigation of the Holy Spirit.

Faith and Warrant

I'm proposing this model as a model of Christian belief's having the sorts of epistemic virtues or the positive epistemic status with which we've been concerned: justification, rationality, and warrant. We've already seen how Christian belief can be justified (above, p. 46). There should be little doubt that Christian belief can be and probably is justified, and justified even for one well acquainted with Enlightenment and postmodern demurrers. If your belief is a result of the internal instigation of the Holy Spirit, it may seem obviously true, even after reflection on the various sorts of objections that have been offered. Clearly one is then violating no intellectual obligations in accepting it. No doubt there are intellectual obligations and duties in the neighborhood; when you note that others disagree with you, for example, perhaps there is a duty to pay attention to them and to their objections, a duty to think again, reflect more deeply, consult others, look for and consider other possible defeaters. But if you have done these things and still find the belief utterly compelling, you are not violating duty or

9. *Most* others: it sometimes happens with human testimony that one person is deputized to speak for another, and in those cases there is the same principal/subordinate structure. See Wolterstorff, *Divine Discourse,* pp. 38ff.

obligation — especially if it seems to you, after reflection, that the teaching in question comes from God himself.

But what about rationality and warrant? And since rationality is included in warrant, we can simplify: what about warrant? The part of Calvin's definition of faith that is especially striking to contemporary ears is that on his account faith is a really special case of *knowledge* ("a sure and certain knowledge"; see also the account of true faith in the Heidelberg Catechism, above, p. 58). Faith is not to be *contrasted* with knowledge: faith (at least in paradigmatic instances) *is* knowledge, knowledge of a certain special kind. It is special in at least two ways. First, in its object: what is allegedly known is (if true) of stunning significance, certainly the most important thing a person could possibly know. But it is also unusual in the way in which that content is known; it is known by way of an extraordinary cognitive process or belief-producing mechanism. The belief-producing process involved is dual, involving both the divinely inspired Scripture (perhaps directly, or perhaps at the head of a testimonial chain), and also the internal instigation of the Holy Spirit. Both involve the special activity of God.

Still, if faith is such an extraordinary way of holding belief, why call it 'knowledge' at all? What about it makes it a case of knowledge? Here we must look a bit more deeply into the model. The believer encounters the great truths of the gospel; by virtue of the activity of the Holy Spirit she comes to see that these things are indeed true. And the first thing to see is that, on this model, faith is indeed a product of a belief-producing *process* or activity, like perception or memory. The activity of the Holy Spirit is or involves a means by which belief, and belief on a certain specific set of topics, is regularly produced in regular ways. In this it resembles memory, perception, reason, sympathy, induction, and other more standard belief-producing processes. (It differs from them in that it is not part of our natural epistemic equipment.)

Now what is required for *knowledge* (as I said above) is that a belief be produced by cognitive faculties or processes that are working properly, in an appropriate epistemic environment, according to a design plan that is aimed at truth, and is furthermore *successfully* aimed at truth. But according to this model, what one believes by faith (the beliefs that constitute faith) meets these four conditions. First, when these beliefs are accepted by faith and result from the internal instigation of the Holy Spirit, they are produced by cognitive processes working properly; they are not produced by way of some cognitive malfunction. The whole process that produces these beliefs is specifically designed by God himself to produce this very effect — just as vision, say, is designed by God to produce a certain kind of perceptual belief. When it does produce this effect, therefore, it is working properly; thus the beliefs in question satisfy the first condition of warrant. Second, according to the model, the environment in which we find ourselves, including the cognitive contamination produced by sin, is precisely the cognitive environment for which this process is designed. Third, the process is designed to produce *true* beliefs.[10] And fourth, according to the model the beliefs they produce — belief in the great things of the gospel — are in fact true; this is a reliable belief-producing process, so that the process in question is *successfully* aimed at the production of true beliefs.

Proper Basicality and the Role of Scripture

One further point: according to the model, Christian belief in the typical case is not the conclusion of an argument or accepted on the evidential basis of other beliefs, or accepted just because it constitutes a good explanation of phenomena of one kind or another. Specific Christian beliefs may indeed constitute excellent explanations of one or another phenomenon (*sin,* for example), but they aren't accepted because they provide such an explanation. Nor are they accepted as the result of historical research. Nor are they accepted as the conclusion of an argument from *religious experience.* According to the model, experience of a certain sort is intimately associated with the formation of warranted Christian belief, but the belief doesn't get its warrant by way of an argument from that experience. It isn't that the believer notes that she or someone else has a certain sort of experience, and somehow concludes that Christian belief must be true. It is rather that (as in the case of perception) the experience is the *occasion* for the formation of the beliefs in question.

In the typical case, therefore, Christian belief is *immediate;* it is formed in the *basic* way. It doesn't proceed by way of an argument. As Jonathan Edwards puts it, "This evidence, that they, that are spiritually

---

10. Though this need not be the *only* purpose involved. Perhaps the beliefs produced have other virtues in addition to truth: perhaps they enable one to stand in a personal relationship with God, to face life's vicissitudes with equanimity, to enjoy the comfort that naturally results from the belief that constitutes faith, and so on.

enlightened, have of the truth of the things of religion, is a kind of intuitive and immediate evidence. They believe the doctrines of God's word to be divine, because they see divinity in them."[11] Christian belief is basic; furthermore Christian belief is *properly* basic, where the propriety in question embraces all three of the epistemic virtues we are considering. On the model the believer is *justified* in accepting these beliefs in the basic way and is *rational* in so doing; still further, the beliefs can have warrant, enough warrant for knowledge, even when they are accepted in that basic way.[12] My Christian belief can have warrant, and warrant sufficient for knowledge, even if I don't know of and cannot make a good historical case for the reliability of the biblical writers or for what they teach. I don't *need* a good historical case for the truth of the central teachings of the gospel in order to be warranted in accepting them. I needn't be able to find a good argument, historical or otherwise, for the resurrection of Jesus Christ, or for his being in fact the divine Son of God, or for the Christian claim that his suffering and death in fact constitutes an atoning sacrifice whereby we can be restored to the right relationship with God. On the model, the warrant for Christian belief doesn't require that I or anyone else have this kind of historical information; the warrant floats free of such questions. It doesn't require to be validated or proved by some source of belief *other* than faith, such as historical investigation.

According to the model, we don't require argument from, for example, historically established premises about the authorship and reliability of the bit of Scripture in question to the conclusion that the bit in question is in fact true. Scripture is self-authenticating in the sense that for belief in the great things of the gospel to be justified, rational, and warranted, no historical evidence and argument for the teaching in question, or for the veracity or reliability or divine character of Scripture (or the part of Scripture in which it is taught), is necessary. The process by which these

11. *The Sermons of Jonathan Edwards: A Reader,* ed. Wilson A. Kimnach et al. (New Haven: Yale University Press, 1999), p. 129.

12. Of course that is not to say that a believer can properly reject proposed defeaters out of hand, without examination (see below, Chapters Eight, Nine, and Ten); nor is she committed to refusing to think she could be wrong. No doubt she can be wrong: that is part of the human condition. If there were a demonstration or a powerful argument from other sources against Christian belief, an argument to which neither she nor the Christian community could see a satisfactory reply, then she might have a problem; this would be a genuine example of a clash between faith and reason. No such demonstration or argument, however, has reared its ugly head.

beliefs have warrant for the believer swings free of those historical and other considerations; these beliefs have warrant in the basic way.

But suppose someone *does* firmly believe these things: isn't this attitude, however it is caused, irrational, contrary to reason? Suppose I read the gospels and come to believe, for example, that Jesus Christ is in fact the divine Son of God and that by his passion, death, and resurrection we human beings, fallen and seriously flawed as we are, can be reconciled to God and have eternal life. Suppose I believe these things without any external evidence. Won't I be leaping to conclusions, forming belief too hastily? What am I really going on, in such a case? Where is my basis, my ground, my evidence? If I have neither propositional evidence nor the sort of ground afforded by perceptual experience, am I not just taking a blind leap? Isn't this leap of faith a leap in the dark? Am I not like someone whose house is on fire and blindly jumps from his third story window, desperately hoping to catch hold of a branch of the tree he knows is somewhere outside the window? And isn't that irresponsible and irrational?

Not at all. Faith, according to the model, is far indeed from being a blind leap; it isn't even remotely like a leap in the dark. Suppose you are descending a glacier at 12,000 feet on Mt. Rainier; there is a nasty whiteout and you can't see more than four feet in front of you. It's getting very late, the wind is rising and the temperature dropping, and you won't survive (you foolishly set out wearing only jeans and a T-shirt) unless you get down before nightfall. So you decide to try to leap the crevasse before you, even though you can't see its other side and haven't the faintest idea how far it is across it. *That's* a leap in the dark. In the case of faith, however, things are wholly different. You might as well claim that a memory belief is a leap in the dark. What makes something a leap in the dark is that the leaper doesn't know and has no firm beliefs about what there is out there in the dark — you might succeed in jumping the crevasse and triumphantly continue your descent, but for all you know you might instead plummet 200 feet into the icy depths of the glacier. You don't really *believe* that you can jump the crevasse (though you don't disbelieve it either); you *hope* you can, and act on what you *do* believe, namely that if you don't jump it, you don't have a chance.

But the case of faith, this sure and certain knowledge, is very different. For the person with faith (at least in the paradigmatic instances) the great things of the gospel seem clearly true, compelling. She finds herself convinced — just as she does in the case of clear memory beliefs or her belief in elementary truths of arithmetic. Phenomenologically, therefore, from the inside, there is no similarity at all to a leap in the dark. Nor, of course, is there (on the model) any similarity from the outside. This is no leap in the dark, not merely because the person with faith is convinced, but also because as a matter of fact the belief in question meets the conditions for rationality and warrant.

One important qualification. It is important to see that the account of belief in the model is an account of *paradigmatic* faith, *ideal* faith, we might say. But it is no part of the model to claim that most cases of faith *are* paradigmatic or ideal. The fact is that the conviction and belief involved in faith come in all degrees of firmness. As Calvin puts it, "in the believing mind certainty is mixed with doubt" and "we are troubled on all sides by the agitation of unbelief" (*Institutes* III.ii.18). In typical cases, as opposed to paradigmatic cases, degree of belief will certainly be less than maximal. Furthermore, degree of belief, on the part of the person who has faith, typically varies from time to time, from circumstance to circumstance. So what can be said is that under certain circumstances what is believed by faith has enough warrant to constitute knowledge; these circumstances, I should guess, are probably not typical, although they are sometimes approached by some Christians part of the time.

To recount the essential features of the model: the internal instigation of the Holy Spirit working in concord with God's teaching in Scripture is a cognitive process or belief-producing mechanism that produces in us the beliefs constituting faith, as well as a host of other beliefs. These beliefs, of course, will seem to the believer to be true: that is part of what it is for them to be *beliefs*. They will have the internal feature of belief, of seeming to be true; and they can have this to various degrees. Second, according to the model, these beliefs will be justified; they will also have at least two further kinds of virtues. In the first place, they are rational, in the sense that the believer's response to the experience she has (given prior belief) is within the range permitted by rationality, that is, by proper function; there is nothing pathological there. And in the second place, the beliefs in question will have warrant: they will be produced by cognitive processes functioning properly in an appropriate environment according to a design plan successfully aimed at the production of true belief.

To be sure, the process in question is not like the ordinary belief-producing mechanisms we have just by virtue of creation; it will be by a special work of the Holy Spirit. Note Hume's sarcastic gibe:

Upon the whole, we may conclude that the *Christian Religion* not only was at first attended with miracles, but even at this day cannot be believed by any reasonable person without one. . . . Whoever is moved by *Faith* to assent to it, is conscious of a continued miracle in his own person, which subverts all the principles of his understanding, and gives him a determination to believe what is most contrary to custom and experience.[13]

According to the model, Hume (sarcasm aside) is partly right: belief in the main lines of the gospel is produced in Christians by a special work of the Holy Spirit, not by the belief-producing faculties and processes with which we were originally created. Further, some of what Christians believe (e.g., that a human being was dead and then arose from the dead) *is* as Hume says, contrary to custom and experience: it seldom happens. Of course it doesn't follow, contrary to Hume's implicit suggestion, that there is anything irrational or contrary to reason in believing it, given the internal instigation of the Holy Spirit.

What I claim for this model is that there aren't any successful philosophical objections to it (in Chapter Seven I'll look into some objections); so far as philosophical considerations go, given the truth of Christian belief, this model, or something like it, is no more than the sober truth. Of course there may be philosophical objections to the truth of Christian belief itself; I shall consider some of them in Chapters Eight through Ten in the guise of defeaters. But the point here is that if Christian belief is true, then it could very well have warrant in the way proposed here. If there are no good philosophical objections to the model, given the *truth* of Christian belief, then any successful objection to the model will also have to be a successful objection to the truth of Christian belief.

We can take the matter a step further. If Christian belief is true, then very likely it does have warrant — if not in the way proposed in the extended A/C model, then in some other similar way. For if Christian belief is true, then, indeed, there is such a person as God, who has created us in his image; we have fallen into sin and require salvation; and the means to such restoral and renewal have been provided in the incarnation, suffering, death, and resurrection of Jesus Christ, the second person of the Trinity. Furthermore, the typical way of appropriating this restoral is by way of faith, which, of course, involves belief in these things — that is, belief in the great things of the gospel. If so, however, God would intend that we be

---

13. *An Enquiry Concerning Human Understanding* (LaSalle, IL: Open Court Publishing, 1956), p. 145.

able to be aware of these truths. And if *that* is so, the natural thing to think is that the cognitive processes that do indeed produce belief in the central elements of the Christian faith are aimed by their designer at producing that belief. Then these beliefs will have warrant.

CHAPTER SIX

Sealed Upon Our Hearts

As we've seen, the extended A/C model shows how Christian belief can have warrant: in the model, Christian belief is produced in the believer by the internal instigation of the Holy Spirit, endorsing the teaching of Scripture, which is itself divinely inspired by the Holy Spirit. The result of the work of the Holy Spirit is *faith* — which, according to both John Calvin and the model, is "a firm and certain knowledge of God's benevolence towards us, founded upon the truth of the freely given promise in Christ, both revealed to our minds and sealed upon our hearts through the Holy Spirit." According to the model, these beliefs enjoy justification, rationality, and warrant. We may therefore say with Calvin that they are "revealed to our minds."

There is more, however; they are also "sealed upon our hearts." What could this mean, and how does it figure into the model? Given that these truths are revealed to our minds, what more could we need? Why must they also be sealed upon our hearts? To answer, suppose we ask whether one could hold the beliefs in question but nonetheless fail to have faith. The traditional Christian answer is, "Well, yes: the demons believe and they shudder" (James 2:19); but the demons do not have faith. So what is the difference? What more is there to faith than belief? What distinguishes the Christian believer from the demons?

According to the model, the shape of the answer is given in the text just mentioned: the demons *shudder*. They *believe* these things, but *hate* them; and they hate God as well. Perhaps they also hope against hope that these things aren't really so, or perhaps they believe them in a self-deceived way. They know of God's power and know that they have no hope of winning any contest with him; nevertheless, they engage in just such a contest, perhaps in that familiar self-deceived condition of really knowing, in one sense, that they couldn't possibly win, while at some other level nevertheless refusing to accept this truth, or hiding it from themselves.

Or perhaps the problem here is not merely cognitive but *affective:* knowing that they couldn't possibly win, they insist on fighting anyway, thinking of themselves as courageously Promethean, as heroically contending against nearly insuperable odds, a condition, they point out, in which God never finds himself, and hence a way in which they can think of themselves as his moral superior. The devils also know of God's wonderful scheme for the salvation of human beings, but they find this scheme — with its mercy and its suffering love — offensive and unworthy. No doubt they endorse Nietzsche's notion that the promotion of Christian love (including the love displayed in the incarnation and atonement) is a strategy on the part of those who are contemptibly weak, whining, resentful, craven, cowardly, servile, duplicitous, and pusillanimous.

The person with faith, however, not only believes the central claims of the Christian faith; she also (paradigmatically) finds the whole scheme of salvation enormously attractive, delightful, moving, a source of amazed wonderment. She is deeply grateful to the Lord for his great goodness and responds to his sacrificial love with love of her own. The difference between believer and devil, therefore, lies at least partly in the area of *affections:* of love and hate, attraction and revulsion, desire and detestation. In traditional categories, the difference lies in the orientation of the *will.* Not primarily in the *executive* function of the will (the function of making decisions, of seeking and avoiding various states of affairs), though of course that is also involved, but in its *affective* function, its function of loving and hating, finding attractive or repellent, approving or disapproving. And the believer, the person with faith, has the right beliefs, but also the right affections. Conversion and regeneration alters affection as well as belief.

According to Calvin, it is the Holy Spirit who is responsible for this sealing upon our hearts of that firm and certain knowledge of God's benevolence toward us; it is the Holy Spirit who is responsible for this renewal and redirection of affections. Calvin is sometimes portrayed as spiritually cold, aloof, bloodless, rationalistic — a person in whom intellect unduly predominates. These charges may (or may not) have some validity with respect to the Reformed scholasticism of a century later; even a cursory examination of Calvin's work, however, reveals that with respect to him they are wildly inaccurate. Calvin's emblem was a flaming heart on an outstretched hand; it bore the motto: *Cor meum quasi immolatum tibi offero,*

Domine.[1] Of the Holy Spirit, he says that "persistently boiling away and burning up our vicious and inordinate desires, he enflames our hearts with the love of God and with zealous devotion." The *Institutes* are throughout aimed at the *practice* of the Christian life (which essentially involves the affections), not at theological theory; the latter enters only in the service of the former.

So the initial difference between believer and demon is partly a matter of affections: the former is inspired to gratitude and love, the latter to fear, hatred, and contempt. The Holy Spirit produces knowledge in the believer; in sealing this knowledge to our hearts, however, it also produces the right affections. Chief among these right affections is love of God — desire for God, desire to know him, to have a personal relationship with him, desire to achieve a certain kind of unity with him, as well as to delight in him, relishing his beauty, greatness, holiness, and the like. There is also trust, approval, gratitude, intention to please, expectation of good things, and much more. Faith, therefore, isn't just a matter of believing certain propositions — not even the momentous propositions of the gospel. Faith is more than belief; in producing faith, the Holy Spirit does more than produce in us the belief that this or that proposition is indeed true. As Aquinas repeats four times in five pages, "the Holy Spirit makes us lovers of God."[2] And according to Martin Luther,

> there are two ways of believing. In the first place I may have faith *concerning* God. This is the case when I hold to be true what is said concerning God. Such faith is on the same level with the assent I give to statements concerning the Turk, the devil and hell. A faith of this kind should be called knowledge or information rather than faith. In the second place there is faith *in*. Such faith is mine when I not only hold to be true what is said concerning God, but when I put my trust in him in such a way as to enter into personal relations with him, believing firmly that I shall find him to be and to do as I have been taught. . . .

---

1. "My heart, as if aflame, I offer to you, O Lord." This particular phenomenology — a phenomenology that is naturally expressed in terms of one's heart being warmed or even aflame — goes back in the Christian tradition at least to the disciples who met the risen Christ on the road to Emmaus: "Then their eyes were opened and they recognized him, and he disappeared from their sight. They asked each other, 'Were not our hearts burning within us while he talked with us on the road and opened the Scriptures to us?'" (Luke 24:31-32).

2. *Summa contra Gentiles,* trans. Charles O'Neil (Notre Dame: University of Notre Dame Press, 1975), Bk. IV, ch. 21, 22 (pp. 122, 125, 126).

The word *in* is well chosen and deserving of due attention. We do not say, I believe God the Father or concerning God the Father, but *in* God the Father, *in* Jesus Christ, and *in* the Holy Spirit.[3]

Jonathan Edwards, one of the great masters of the interior life and a peerless student of the religious affections, concurs with Calvin that true religion is more than just right belief. Indeed, according to him, true religion is *first* a matter of having the right affections: "True religion, in great part, consists in holy affections."[4] "The Holy Scriptures do everywhere place religion very much in the affections; such as fear, hope, love, hatred, desire, joy, sorrow, gratitude, compassion and zeal" (p. 272). Mere knowledge isn't enough for true religion:

There is a distinction to be made between a mere notional understanding, wherein the mind only beholds things in the exercise of a speculative faculty; and the sense of the heart, wherein the mind doesn't only speculate and behold, but relishes and feels. That sort of knowledge, by which a man has a sensible perception of amiableness and loathsomeness, or of sweetness and nauseousness, is not just the same sort of knowledge with that, by which he knows what a triangle is, and what a square is. The one is mere speculative knowledge; the other sensible knowledge, in which more than the mere intellect is concerned; the heart is the proper subject of it, or the soul as a being that not only beholds, but has inclination, and is pleased or displeased. (p. 272)

Edwards doesn't think true religion is *just* or *merely* a matter of affections, of loves and hates, as if belief and understanding had no role to play: "Holy affections are not heat without light; but evermore arise from some information of the understanding, some spiritual instruction that the mind receives, some light or actual knowledge" (p. 266). Still, true religion *primarily* involves (so he seems to say) the affections. In particular, true religion involves love: "all true religion summarily consists in the love of

3. *Luther's Catechetical Writings,* trans. J. N. Lenker, 2 vols. (Minneapolis: Lutheran Press, 1907), 1:203, quoted in H. R. Niebuhr, *Faith on Earth* (New Haven: Yale University Press, 1989), p. 9. Consider also Pascal: "So those to whom God has imparted religion through the feeling of the heart are very fortunate and justly convinced" (*Pensées,* trans. M. Turnell [London: Harvill Press, 1962], p. 282).

4. *A Treatise Concerning Religious Affections,* ed. John E. Smith (New Haven: Yale University Press, 1959 [1746]), p. 95. Page references to *Religious Affections* are to this edition.

divine things" (p. 271). And love brings other affections in its train: "love to God," he says, "causes a man to delight in the thoughts of God, and to delight in the presence of God and to desire conformity to God, and the enjoyment of God" (p. 208); elsewhere, he adds that one who loves God will also delight in contemplating the great things of the gospel, taking pleasure in them, finding them attractive, marvelous, winsome (p. 250). Further, one who thus delights in the great truths of the gospel may find himself disgusted by various attempts to trade that splendidly rich and powerful gospel for cheap and trivial substitutes. Still further, acquiring the right affections enables one to see the true heinousness of sin: "He who sees the beauty of holiness, must necessarily see the hatefulness of sin, its contrary" (p. 274); and he who *sees* the hatefulness of sin (in himself and others) will also (given proper function) *hate* it.

Conversion, therefore, is fundamentally a turning of the will, a healing of the disorder of affection that afflicts us. It is a turning away from love of self, from thinking of oneself as the chief being of the universe, to love of God. But what is this love of God like, and how shall we understand it? William James, that cultured, sophisticated New England Victorian gentleman, notes the throbbing elements of longing, yearning, desire, in the writings of Teresa of Avila, looks down his cultivated nose, and finds all that a bit, well, *tasteless,* a bit *déclassé.* Sniffs James, "In the main her idea of religion seems to have been that of an endless amatory flirtation . . . between the devotee and the deity."[5]

Here the joke is on James. There is an intimate and longstanding connection between eros and developed spirituality. And here we should not think of eros as merely a matter of romantic or sexual love. Thinking more broadly, eros is instead a genus of which romantic love is a species, a kind of love of which romantic and sexual love is a special case. The essence of eros, as I'm thinking of it, is longing, desire, a desire for some kind of union.

The Bible is full of expressions of that longing, yearning, *Sehnsucht,* desire; the Psalms are particularly rich in such expressions of eros:

> My soul yearns, even faints, for the courts of the Lord; my heart and
> my flesh cry out for the living God. (Ps. 84:2)
> O God, you are my God, earnestly I seek you; my soul thirsts for you,
> my body longs for you. (Ps. 63:1)

5. *The Varieties of Religious Experience* (New York: Longmans, Green, 1902), p. 340.

One thing have I desired of the Lord, that I will seek after; that I . . .
  behold the beauty of the Lord. (Ps. 27:4 KJV)
As the deer pants for streams of water, so my soul pants for you, O
  God. My soul thirsts for God, for the living God. (Ps. 42:1-2)
I open my mouth and pant, longing for your commands. (Ps. 119:131)

This love for God isn't like, say, an inclination to spend the afternoon
organizing your stamp collection. It is longing, filled with desire and yearning; and it is physical as well as spiritual: "my body longs for you, my soul
pants for you." Although eros is broader than sexual love, it is analogous
to the latter. There is a powerful desire for *union* with God, the oneness
Christ refers to in John 17. Of course sexual love is not the only analogue.
Another equally close analogue would be love between parent and small
child; and this kind of love too is often employed in Scripture as a figure for
love of God — both God's love for us and ours for him. Here too, there is a
kind of longing, yearning, desire for closeness; think of the longing in the
homesickness of an eight-year-old obliged to leave home for the summer,
or in the love of a mother for her hurt and suffering child.

There are other manifestations of the same kind of desire for union.
Consider the haunting, supernal beauty of the prairie on an early morning in June, or the glorious but slightly menacing aspect of the Cathedral
group in the Grand Tetons, or the gleaming splendor of Mount Shuksan
and Mount Baker from Skyline Ridge, or the timeless crash and roar of
the surf, or the melting sweetness of Mozart's *"Dona Nobis Pacem,"* or the
incredible grace, beauty, and power of an ice-skating routine or of a kickoff
returned for ninety-eight yards. In each, there is a kind of yearning, something perhaps a little like nostalgia, or perhaps homesickness, a longing
for one knows not what. This longing is different from sexual eros, though
perhaps connected with it at a deep level. In these cases it isn't easy to say
with any precision what the longing is a longing *for,* but it can seem to be
for a sort of union: it's as if you want to be absorbed into the music, to become part of the ocean, to be at one with the landscape. You would love to
climb that mountain, certainly, but that isn't enough; you also somehow
want to become one with it, to become part of it, or to have it, or its beauty,
or this particular aspect of it, somehow become part of your very soul.[6]

6. Compare C. S. Lewis: our "inconsolable secret" is that "We do not want merely to
see beauty, though, God knows, even that is bounty enough. We want something else which
can hardly be put into words — to be united with the beauty we see, to pass into it, to receive

Of course you can't; you remain unsatisfied. Jean-Paul Sartre says that man (and I doubt that he meant to single out just males) is *"de trop,"* too much; perhaps the truth is more like "not enough." He also says that man is a "useless passion." What he should have said is that man is an *unfulfilled* passion. When confronted with beauty, it is never enough; we are never really satisfied; there is more beyond, a more that we yearn for, but can only dimly conceive. We are limited to mere fleeting glimpses of the real satisfaction — unfulfilled until filled with the love of God. These longings too are types of longing for God; and the brief but joyous partial fulfillments are a type and foretaste of the fulfillment enjoyed by those who "glorify God and enjoy him forever."[7]

These kinds of longing, desire, eros, point to something deeper. They are a sign or type of a deeper reality, a kind of love for God of which we now have no more than hints and intimations. But they are also a sign, symbol, or type of *God's* love — not just of the love God's children will someday have for *him* but of the love he also has for *them*. As we noted above, Scripture regularly compares God's love for his people and Christ's love for his church to the love of a groom for his new bride.

Now a widely shared traditional view of God has been that he is impassible, that is, without desire or feeling or passion, unable to feel sorrow at the sad condition of his world and the suffering of his children, and equally unable to feel joy, delight, longing, or yearning. The reason for so thinking, roughly, is that in the tradition originating in Greek philosophy, passions were thought of (what else?) as *passive,* something that *happens* to you, something you undergo, rather than something you actively *do.* You are *subject to* and *undergo* anger, love, joy, and all the rest. God, however, doesn't 'undergo' anything at all; he acts, and is never merely passive; and he isn't subject to anything.

As far as eros is concerned, furthermore, there is an additional reason for thinking that it isn't part of God's life: longing and yearning signify need and *incompleteness.* One who yearns for something doesn't yet have it, and needs it, or at any rate thinks he needs it; God is of course paradigmatically complete and needs nothing beyond himself. How, then, could he be subject to eros? God's love, according to this tradition, is exclusively *agape,*

---

it into ourselves, to bathe in it, to become part of it" (*The Weight of Glory* [London: Society for Promoting Christian Knowledge, 1942], p. 8).

7. See the first question and answer of the Westminster Confession: "Question: What is the chief and highest end of man? Answer: Man's chief and highest end is to glorify God, and fully to enjoy him forever."

benevolence,[8] a completely other-regarding, magnanimous love in which there is mercy but no element of desire. God loves us, but there is nothing we can do for him; he wishes nothing from us.

On this particular point I think we must take leave of the tradition; this is one of those places where it has paid too much attention to Greek philosophy and too little to the Bible. I believe God can and does suffer; his capacity for suffering exceeds ours in the same measure that his knowledge exceeds ours. Christ's suffering was no charade; he was prepared to endure the agonies of the cross and of hell itself ("My God, my God, why have you forsaken me?").[9] God the Father was prepared to endure the anguish of seeing his Son, the second person of the Trinity, consigned to the bitterly cruel and shameful death of the cross. And isn't the same true for other passions? "There is more rejoicing in heaven over one sinner who repents than over ninety-nine righteous persons who do not need to repent" (Luke 15:7); is God himself to be excluded from this rejoicing?

Similarly for eros: "As a bridegroom rejoices over his bride, so will your God rejoice over you" (Isa. 62:5). The bridegroom rejoicing over his bride doesn't love her with a merely agapeic love. He isn't like her benevolent elder brother (although Christ is also said to be our elder brother). He desires and longs for something outside himself, namely union with his beloved. The church is the *bride* of Christ, not his little sister. These scriptural images imply that God isn't impassive, and that his love for us is not exclusively agapeic. They suggest that God's love for his people involves an element of desire: he desires the right kind of response from us, and union with us, just as we desire union with him.

We can take this one step further. According to Jonathan Edwards, "The infinite happiness of the Father consists in the enjoyment of His Son."[10] This presumably isn't agape. It doesn't involve an element of mercy, as in

8. See Anders Nygren, *Agape and Eros,* trans. Philip S. Watson (New York: Macmillan, 1969). The Swedish original edition was published in 1935.

9. Can we say that Christ *qua* human being (according to his human nature) suffered while Christ *qua* divine (according to his divine nature) did not? This is hardly the place to try to address a question as ancient and deep as this one, but I'm inclined to think this suggestion incoherent. There is this person, the second person of the divine Trinity who became incarnate. It is this person who suffers; if there really were *two* centers of consciousness here, one suffering and the other not, there would be two persons here (one human and one divine) rather than the one person who is both human and divine. See my "On Heresy, Mind, and Truth," *Faith and Philosophy* 16, no. 2 (1999): 182.

10. "An Essay on the Trinity," in *Treatise on Grace and Other Posthumously Published Writings,* ed. Paul Helm (Cambridge: James Clarke, 1971), p. 105.

his love for us. It is, instead, a matter of God's taking enormous pleasure, enjoyment, delight, happiness in the Son. Given the necessary existence of the Father and the Son, and given that they have their most important properties essentially, there is no way in which God could be deprived of the Son;[11] but if *(per impossible)* he were, it would occasion inconceivable sadness. The love in question is eros, not agape.[12] It is a desire for union that is continually, eternally, and joyfully satisfied. And our being created in his image involves our capacity for eros and for love of what is genuinely lovable, as well as our capacity for knowledge and our ability to act.

Accordingly, the eros in our lives is a sign or a symbol of God's erotic love as well. Human erotic love is a sign of something deeper, something so deep that it is uncreated, an original and permanent and necessarily present feature of the universe. Eros undoubtedly characterizes many creatures other than human beings; no doubt much of the living universe shares this characteristic. More important, all of us creatures with eros reflect and partake in this profound divine property. So the most fundamental reality here is the love displayed by and in God: love within the Trinity.[13] This love is a matter of perceiving and desiring and enjoying union with something valuable, in this case, Someone of supreme value. And God's love for us is manifested in his generously inviting us into this charmed circle (though not, of course, to ontological equality), thus satisfying the deepest longings of our souls.

In sum, then: according to the model, faith is a matter of sure and certain knowledge, both revealed to our minds and sealed to our hearts.

---

11. And this is the answer to one of the traditional arguments for the conclusion that God has no passions: the Father and the Son do indeed *need* each other, but it is a need that is necessarily and eternally fulfilled.

12. "So when we say that God loves his Son, we are not talking about a love that is self-denying, sacrificial, or merciful. We are talking about a love of delight and pleasure. . . . He is well-pleased with his Son. His soul delights in the Son! When he looks at his Son he enjoys and admires and cherishes and prizes and relishes what he sees" (John Piper, *The Pleasures of God* [Portland: Multnomah, 1991], p. 31).

13. The thought that God is triune distinguishes Christianity from other theistic religions; here we see a way in which this doctrine makes a real difference, in that it recognizes eros and love for others at the most fundamental level of reality. Does this suggest that we should lean toward a *social* conception of the Trinity, the conception of Gregory and the Cappadocian fathers, rather than the Augustinian conception, which flirts with modalism? See Cornelius Plantinga Jr., "Social Trinity and Tritheism," in *Trinity, Incarnation, and Atonement,* ed. Ronald Feenstra and Cornelius Plantinga Jr. (Notre Dame: University of Notre Dame Press, 1989).

This sealing, according to the model, consists in having the right sorts of affections; in essence, it consists in loving God above all and one's neighbor as oneself. There is an intimate relation between revealing and sealing, knowledge and affection, intellect and will; they cooperate in a deep and complex and intimate way in the person of faith. And the love involved is, in part, erotic; it involves that longing and yearning with which we are all familiar. Finally, love between human beings — between men and women, between parents and children, among friends — is a sign or type of something deeper: mature human love for God, on the one hand, and, on the other, the love of God displayed both among the members of the Trinity and in God's love for his children.

CHAPTER SEVEN

Objections

The extended Aquinas/Calvin (A/C) model is designed to show that and how specifically Christian belief can have justification, rationality, and warrant. According to the model, we human beings have fallen into sin, a grievous condition from which we cannot extricate ourselves. Jesus Christ, both a human being and the divine Son of God, made atonement for our sin by way of his suffering and death, thus making it possible for us to stand in the right relationship to God. The Bible is (among other things) a written communication from God to us human beings, proclaiming this good news. Because of our fallen condition, however, we need more than this information: we also need a change of heart. This is provided by the internal instigation of the Holy Spirit (IIHS); he both enables us to see the truth of the great things of the gospel and turns our affections in the right direction. The process whereby we come to believe those things, therefore, satisfies the conditions for both rationality and warrant.

In this chapter I'll consider a couple of objections to the model, taken in this way as an argument for the conclusion that Christian belief can have rationality and warrant.

Warrant and the Argument from Religious Experience

First, a number of thinkers consider the question whether Christian belief can be justified or warranted by way of *religious experience;* they go on to argue that it cannot. Now it isn't clear whether or not, on the model, Christian belief gets its warrant from or through religious experience. Suppose my belief in the great things of the gospel is a result of IIHS; is it then true that this belief gets its warrant through religious experience? Maybe so, maybe not; it isn't clear, and as far as the model is concerned, it could go either way. Technically speaking, therefore, these objections wouldn't apply to my claims about how it can be that such belief has warrant. For the purpose of considering these objections, however, let's concede what may well be false — namely that (on the model) these beliefs *do* get their warrant from experience. Then at any rate we can see the objections as initially relevant.

Now this first objection is really less an objection, so it seems to me, than a confusion, a failure to make an important distinction.

According to the late J. L. Mackie,

> an experience may have a real object: we ordinarily suppose our normal perceptual experience to be or to include awareness of independently existing material spatio-temporal things. The question then is whether specifically religious experiences should be taken to have real objects, to give us genuine information about independently existing supernatural entities or spiritual beings.[1]

So far so good: this is the question whether religious experience can or does provide warrant for belief in "independently existing supernatural entities or spiritual beings" such as God.

But Mackie goes on:

> Whether their content [i.e., the content of religious experiences] has any objective truth is the crucial further question. . . . The issue is whether the hypothesis that there objectively is a something more gives a better explanation of the whole range of phenomena than can be given without it. (p. 183)

Mackie concludes his examination of the possible warrant conferred by religious experience with these words:

> if the religious experiences do not yield any argument for a further supernatural reality, and if, as we have seen in previous chapters, there is no other good argument for such a conclusion, then these experi-

1. *The Miracle of Theism* (Oxford: Clarendon, 1982), p. 178. Page references to Mackie are to this work.

ences include in their content beliefs that are probably false and in any case unjustified. [I take it 'unjustified,' here, means 'without warrant.'] (p. 186)

Here Mackie assumes that theistic (or other religious) belief could get warrant through or by way of religious experience only if there is a good argument from the existence and character of that experience to the existence of God (or "something more"). Mackie doesn't *argue* for this claim, simply taking it utterly for granted that the only way a belief (or at any rate a religious or theistic belief) could *possibly* receive warrant from experience would be by way of an implicit argument from the existence and properties of that experience to the truth of the belief in question.

But why think a thing like that? It certainly isn't self-evident. In fact, once we explicitly raise the question, it looks extremely problematic. Presumably one wouldn't want to say that *perceptual* beliefs get warrant from experience only if there is a good argument from the existence of perceptual experience to the truth of perceptual beliefs; if not, however, what is the reason for saying it in the case of theistic or Christian belief?

Mackie makes this assumption, I believe, because he makes another: that theistic and Christian belief is or is relevantly like a *scientific hypothesis* — something like special relativity, for example, or quantum mechanics, or the theory of evolution. Still speaking of whether theistic belief can receive warrant by way of religious experience, he (characteristically) remarks: "Here, as elsewhere, the supernaturalist hypothesis fails because there is an adequate and much more economical naturalistic alternative" (p. 198). This remark is relevant only if we think of belief in God as or as like a sort of scientific *hypothesis,* a *theory* designed to explain some body of evidence, and acceptable or warranted to the degree that it explains that evidence. On this way of looking at the matter, there is a relevant body of evidence shared by believer and unbeliever alike; theism is one hypothesis designed to explain that body of evidence, and naturalism is another; and theism has warrant only to the extent that it is a good explanation thereof, or at any rate a better explanation than naturalism.

But why should we think of theism like this? Why should we think of it as a kind of hypothesis, a sort of incipient science? Consider the extended A/C model. On that model, it is not that one notes the experiences (whatever exactly they are) connected with the operation of the *sensus divinitatis,* and then makes a quick inference to the existence of God. One doesn't argue thus: "I am aware of the beauty and majesty of the heavens (or of my own guilt, or that I am in danger, or of the glorious beauty of the morning, or of my good circumstances): therefore there is such a person as God." The Christian doesn't argue: "I find myself loving and delighting in the great things of the gospel and inclined to believe them; therefore they are true." Those would be silly arguments; fortunately they are neither invoked nor needed. The experiences and beliefs involved in the operation of the *sensus divinitatis* and IIHS serve as *occasions* for theistic belief, not *premises* for an argument to it.

The same holds for, say, memory beliefs. Obviously one could take a Mackie-like view here as well. One could hold that our beliefs about the past are really like scientific hypotheses, designed to explain such present phenomena as (among other things) apparent memories, and if there were a more "economical" explanation of these phenomena that did not postulate past facts, then our usual beliefs in the past would have no warrant. But of course this is merely fantastic; we don't in fact accept memory beliefs as hypotheses to explain present experience at all. Everyone, even small children and others with no interest in explaining anything, accepts memory beliefs. We all remember such things as what we had for breakfast, and we never or almost never propose such beliefs as good explanations of present experience and phenomena. And the same holds for theism and Christian belief in the suggested model.

Mackie apparently believes that (1) theistic belief is or is relevantly like a quasi-scientific hypothesis designed to explain religious experience (perhaps among other things).

This explains why he believes (2), that is, that theistic belief can get no warrant from religious experience unless there is a good argument from premises reporting the experiences to the existence of God. As we have seen, however, (1) is false.

Well, perhaps Mackie would insist on (2) even if it is clear that Christians do *not* take belief in God or Christian belief generally as hypotheses; perhaps he would nonetheless insist that the only way in which such belief could *possibly* get warrant would be by being successful quasi-scientific hypotheses.

But precisely this is what is refuted by the A/C and extended A/C models. These models show how it is clearly possible that theistic and Christian belief have warrant, but not by way of being hypotheses that nicely explain a certain range of data. For if Christian belief is, in fact, true, then obviously there could be such cognitive processes as the *sensus divinitatis* and IIHS or faith. As we saw, beliefs produced by these processes would meet the conditions necessary and sufficient for having warrant: they would be the result of cognitive faculties functioning properly in a congenial epistemic environment according to a design plan successfully aimed at truth. Hence it is plainly false that Christian belief has warrant (and could constitute knowledge) only if we *also* have a good argument from the existence of the experiences involved in the operation of IIHS to the truth of Christian belief; and the same point holds for theistic belief and the *sensus divinitatis*.

Why suppose that if God proposes to enable us to have knowledge of a certain sort, he must arrange things in such a way that we can see an argumentative connection between the experiences involved in the cognitive processes he selects, and the truth of the beliefs these processes produce? That requirement is both entirely gratuitous and also false, since it doesn't hold for such splendid examples of sources of knowledge as perception, memory, and *a priori* intuition.

What Can Experience Show?

A second objection is that Christian and theistic belief could never receive warrant from religious experience because religious experience could never indicate or show anything as *specific* as that there is such a person as God — let alone such beliefs as that in Christ, God was reconciling the world to himself. How could experience of any sort reveal the existence of a being who is omniscient, omnipotent, wholly good, and a fitting object of worship? How could it reveal that there is only *one* being like that? How could experience carry that kind of information? John Mackie is a spokesman for this objection too:

> Religious experience is also essentially incapable of supporting any argument for the traditional central doctrines of theism. Nothing in an experience as such could reveal a creator of the world, or omnipotence, or omniscience, or perfect goodness, or eternity, or even that there is just one god. (p. 182)

Now why would Mackie say a thing like that? And what precisely does he mean? For present purposes, suppose we restrict ourselves to the experience involved in the operation of the *sensus divinitatis*. I *think* what Mackie means is this: given any course of experience, religious or otherwise — that is, given any course of sensuous imagery, affective experience, and inclinations to believe I might have — that experience could be exactly as it is and there be no omnipotent being, or omniscient being, or perfectly good or eternal being. My experience could be precisely what it is, and there be no such person as God or anyone or anything at all like God. I could feel the very way I do feel, and there be no God.

I *think* this is what he means; I can't be sure. That is because it seems of only dubious relevance. Perhaps it is true that my experience could be just as it is and there be no such person as God; perhaps the existence and character of my experience don't entail the existence of God. What follows? Why should it follow that my experience cannot reveal a creator of the world or an omnipotent or omniscient being?

Consider an analogy: we all ordinarily think we have existed for many years (or, in the case of you younger readers, many months). It is logically possible, however, that I should have existed for only a microsecond or two, displaying all the temporally specific properties I do in fact display. Then I wouldn't have such properties as being more than sixty years old or being responsible for something that happened ten minutes ago, although I would have such properties as *thinking* that I am more than sixty years old and that I am responsible for something that happened ten minutes ago.

Not only is this logically possible, it is also compatible with the existence and character of all of my present experience. It is not compatible with my *beliefs,* of course (in that I believe I've existed for quite a while); still, it is compatible with the *existence* of those beliefs. It is possible that I should have precisely the beliefs and experiences I now have, despite my having come into existence just a second or less ago. (In fact that is precisely what happens, according to those who think the word 'I', as I use it, denotes something like a momentary person stage.[2]) For any course of experience and any set of beliefs I might have at this very moment, it is possible that I have that experience and hold those beliefs but nonetheless have existed for only a second or less.

Does it follow that nothing in my experience can reveal that I have existed for more than the last second or so? Certainly not. There isn't the slightest reason to believe that if experience can reveal *p*, then the existence of that experience (or the proposition that it occurs) must entail the truth of *p*. There is no reason to think that if experience can reveal a

---

2. See my *Warrant and Proper Function* (Oxford: Oxford University Press, 1993), pp. 5off.

proposition *p,* then that experience must be such that it (logically) cannot so much as exist if *p* is false. For consider perception, and consider my experience on an occasion when I see a horse. It is compatible with those experiences that there be no horse there then, that there be no horses at all, that there be no material objects that exist when I am not undergoing those experiences, and, indeed, that there be no material objects at all. Does it follow that perceptual experience doesn't reveal an external world? Does it follow that I can't know from or by way of my experience that there is a horse in my backyard? Surely not; that would be a leap of magnificent (if grotesque) proportions.

Well then, how *does* perceptual experience reveal an external world — a horse, say? When I perceive a horse, I am the subject of experiences of various kinds: sensuous imagery (I am appeared to in a certain complicated and hard-to-describe fashion) and also, ordinarily, affective experience (perhaps I am frightened by the horse, or feel a certain admiration for it, or delight in its speed and strength or whatever). There is also what we might call doxastic[3] experience. When I perceive a horse, there is that sensuous and affective experience, but also the feeling, experience, intimation with respect to a certain proposition (the proposition *I see a horse*) that *that* proposition is true, right, to be believed, the way things really are. This doxastic experience plays a crucial role in perception. How *does* perceptual experience teach me that there is a horse in my backyard? By way of this belief's being occasioned (in part) by the experience, and by way of the belief's having warrant — being produced by properly functioning cognitive faculties in an appropriate epistemic environment, according to a design plan successfully aimed at truth. So can I know from my experience that there is a horse there? Certainly. Knowing such a thing from one's experience is forming the belief that a horse is there in response to the sensuous and doxastic experience, the belief's being formed under the conditions that confer warrant. The fact is, this happens all the time.

My point here is not that, in fact, people *do* tell from their experience such things as that there is a horse in the backyard, but rather that this is *possible.* More exactly, my point is that your seeing a horse in your backyard (thus determining by experience that there is a horse there) is not precluded by the fact that your experience is logically compatible with there being no horse there (or anywhere else). Your experience is logically compatible with there being no horse there: fair enough; but it simply

---

3. From the Greek word *doxa,* meaning belief or opinion.

doesn't follow that you can't tell by experience that there *is* a horse there. (How else would you tell? Deduce it from first principles and self-evident truths?) That's the way it is with *horses;* can I also tell from my experience that *I* have existed for more than a microsecond or so? Certainly. I do this by remembering, for example, that I had breakfast much more than a microsecond ago and that I went to college embarrassingly long ago. True, my experience here (in particular, my doxastic experience) is compatible with its being the case that I have existed for only a microsecond; it simply doesn't follow that I can't tell by experience that I have existed for at least a good hour, say. I determine by experience that I have existed for more than a microsecond if the belief that I did something more than a microsecond ago is occasioned by my experience (doxastic and otherwise) and if that belief is formed under conditions that confer warrant upon it. This happens often: so we often tell (by experience) that we have existed for more than a microsecond.

And of course the same goes for religious experience and theistic belief. True: the existence of the experiences that go with the operation of the *sensus divinitatis* is compatible with there being no omnipotent, omniscient, wholly good creator of the universe. It doesn't follow from that, however, that we can't know — and know, broadly speaking, by experience — that there is such a person. For here, as elsewhere, there is doxastic experience: the belief that there is an almighty person to whom I owe allegiance and obedience just seems right, proper, true, the way things are. And one tells by experience that there is such a person if (1) the beliefs in question are formed in response to the experiences (doxastic and otherwise) that go with the operation of the *sensus divinitatis* and (2) those beliefs are formed under the conditions of warrant. Those beliefs can have warrant, and enough warrant to constitute knowledge, even if the existence of those experiences is compatible with the denials of those beliefs. The same goes for beliefs in the great things of the gospel: they too can have warrant (and warrant sufficient for knowledge), even if, in fact, the existence of the experiences accompanying the IIHS is compatible with the falsehood of those beliefs.

The A/C and extended A/C models are designed to show how it could be that theistic and Christian beliefs can have warrant. We've just looked at a couple of characteristic objections leading to the conclusion that these models can't do what they are designed to do. What we've also seen is that these objections fail. Are there are other sensible objections? Perhaps so; it will be time to consider them when (and if) they arise.

But of course, even if Christian and theistic belief *can* have warrant, perhaps they don't in fact have that valuable property: perhaps there are *defeaters*. In the next chapter we'll turn to that topic.

CHAPTER EIGHT

Defeaters? Historical Biblical Criticism

So far I've argued that Christian belief — the full panoply of Christian belief, including Trinity, incarnation, atonement, resurrection — can, if true, have warrant. If Christian belief is true, Christians can *know* that it is. The extended Aquinas/Calvin (A/C) model shows how it can be that beliefs of these sorts do indeed have warrant. On this model, Christian belief does not come by way of arguments from other beliefs. Rather, the fundamental idea is that God provides us human beings with faculties or belief-producing processes that yield these beliefs and are successfully aimed at the truth; when they work the way they were designed to in the sort of environment for which they were designed, the result is knowledge or warranted belief.

Of course this hardly settles the issue as to whether Christian belief (even if true) has or can have warrant in the circumstances in which most of us actually find ourselves. Someone might put it like this: "Well, perhaps these beliefs can have warrant and constitute knowledge: there are circumstances in which this can happen. Most of us, however — for example, most of those who read this book — are not in those circumstances. What you have argued so far is only that theistic and Christian belief (taken in the basic way) can have warrant, *absent defeaters*. But defeaters are not absent."

The claim is that there are serious defeaters for Christian belief: propositions we know or believe that make Christian belief — at any rate, Christian belief held in the basic way and with anything like sufficient firmness to constitute knowledge — *irrational* and hence unwarranted. Philip Quinn, for example, believes that for "intellectually sophisticated adults in our culture" there are important defeaters for belief in God — at least if, as in the A/C model, held in the basic way. As a result, belief in God held in the basic way, as in the model, is for the most part irrational: "I conclude that many, perhaps most, intellectually sophisticated adults in our culture are seldom if ever in conditions which are right for [theistic beliefs] to be properly basic for them."[1]

Defeaters

Is Quinn right? To answer, we must first look into a preliminary question: What is a defeater? Here some examples would be useful. I see (at a hundred yards) what I take to be a sheep in a field and, naturally enough, form the belief that there is a sheep in the field; I know that you are the owner of the field; the next day you tell me that there are no sheep in that field, although you own a dog who looks like a sheep at a hundred yards and who frequents the field. Then (in the absence of special circumstances) I have a defeater for the belief that there was a sheep in that field and will, if rational, no longer hold that belief.

Another kind of defeater: you enter a factory and see an assembly line on which there are a number of widgets, all of which look red. You form the belief that they are red. Then along comes the shop superintendent, who informs you that the widgets are being irradiated by red and infrared light, a process that makes it possible to detect otherwise undetectable hair-line cracks. You then have a defeater for your belief that the widget you are looking at is red. In this case, what you learn is not that the defeated belief is false (you aren't told that this widget isn't red); what you learn, rather, is something that undercuts your grounds or reasons for thinking it red. (You realize that it would look red even if it weren't.)

Defeaters, therefore, are reasons for giving up a belief *B* you hold. If they are also reasons for believing *B* false, they are rebutting defeaters; if they *aren't* reasons for believing *B* false, they are undercutting defeaters. Acquiring a defeater for a belief puts you in a position in which you can't rationally continue to hold the belief.

Defeaters depend on the rest of what you know and believe. Whether a belief *A* is a defeater for a belief *B* doesn't depend merely on my current

1. "In Search of the Foundations of Theism," *Faith and Philosophy* 2, no. 4 (1985): 481. See my "The Foundations of Theism: A Reply," *Faith and Philosophy* 3, no. 3 (1986): 298ff.; and Quinn's rejoinder, "The Foundations of Theism Again," in *Rational Faith: Catholic Responses to Reformed Epistemology,* ed. Linda Zagzebski (Notre Dame: University of Notre Dame Press, 1993), pp. 14ff.

experience; it also depends on what other beliefs I have, and how firmly I hold them. Return to the case where your saying that there are no sheep in the field is a defeater for my belief that I see a sheep there. This depends on my assuming you to be trustworthy, at least on this occasion and on this topic. By contrast, if I know you are a notorious practical joker especially given to misleading people about sheep, what you say will not constitute a defeater; the same goes if I am inspecting the sheep through powerful binoculars and clearly see that it is a sheep, or if there is someone I trust standing right in front of the sheep, who tells me by cell phone that it is indeed a sheep.

One more example of a defeater, this one historically famous. The mathematician and philosopher Gottlob Frege (1848-1925) once believed that

(F) For every condition or property *P*, there exists the set of just those things that have *P*.

The philosopher Bertrand Russell (1872-1970) wrote him a letter, pointing out that (F) has very serious problems. First, there is the property or condition of being non-self-membered; that property is had by every set that is not a member of itself. (For example, the set of horses is not itself a horse; hence that set is not a member of itself.) But then by (F) there exists the set of non-self-membered sets. This set, however, inconsiderately fails to exist. That is because if it did exist, it would be a member of itself if and only if it were *not* a member of itself. From that it follows that it would both exemplify itself and fail to exemplify itself (think about it), which is wholly unacceptable behavior for a set. Before he realized this problem with (F), Frege did not have a defeater for it. Once he understood Russell's letter, however, he did; and the defeater was just his newly acquired belief that (F), together with the truth that there is such a condition as being non-self-membered, entails a contradiction.

Now that we are clear about defeaters and their devious ways, I'll turn in the next three chapters to three proposed defeaters for Christian belief, and argue that in each case they don't in fact serve as defeaters. In this chapter, I'll argue that contemporary historical biblical criticism ('higher criticism') doesn't serve as a defeater for Christian belief, even when its alleged results do not support Christian belief and, indeed, even when they go counter to it. Next, in Chapter Nine, I'll examine (and find wanting) the claim that the facts of religious pluralism constitute a defeater for Christian belief. Finally, in Chapter Ten, I'll consider what has often been seen as the most formidable challenge of all to Christian belief: the facts of suffering and evil. This challenge too, I'll argue, does not as such constitute a defeater for Christian belief.

Two Kinds of Scripture Scholarship

On the extended A/C model, Scripture, the Bible, is a message from the Lord. According to the model, Scripture is *perspicuous:* the main lines of its teaching — creation, sin, incarnation, atonement, resurrection, eternal life — can be understood and grasped and properly accepted by anyone of normal intelligence and ordinary training. As Jonathan Edwards said, the Housatonic Indians can easily grasp and properly appropriate this message; a PhD in theology or biblical history is not necessary.

Underlying this point is a second: there is available a source of warranted true belief, a way of coming to see the truth of these teachings, that is quite independent of historical study: Scripture/the internal instigation of the Holy Spirit/faith. By virtue of this process, an ordinary Christian, one quite innocent of historical studies, the ancient languages, the intricacies of textual criticism, the depths of theology, and all the rest can nevertheless come to know that these things are, indeed, true. Furthermore, this knowledge need not trace back (by way of testimony, for example) to knowledge on the part of someone who *does* have this specialized training. Neither the Christian community nor the ordinary Christian is at the mercy of the expert here; they can know these truths directly.

Nevertheless, of course, the serious and scholarly study of the Bible is of first importance for Christians. The roll call of those who have pursued this project is maximally impressive: Chrysostom, Augustine, Aquinas, Calvin, and Jonathan Edwards, just for starters. These people and their successors begin from the idea that Scripture is divinely inspired in such a way that the Bible constitutes a divine revelation, a special message from God to humankind; they then try to ascertain the Lord's teaching in the whole of Scripture or (more likely) a given bit.

Since the Enlightenment, however, another kind of scriptural scholarship has come into view. Variously called 'higher criticism', 'historical criticism', 'biblical criticism', or 'historical critical scholarship', this variety of scriptural scholarship brackets or sets aside what is known by faith and aims to proceed 'scientifically', strictly on the basis of reason. I'll call it 'historical biblical criticism' — HBC for short. Scripture scholarship of this sort brackets (i.e., sets aside) the belief that the Bible is a special word from the Lord, as well as any other belief accepted on the basis of faith.

Now it often happens that the declarations of those who pursue this latter kind of Scripture scholarship are in apparent conflict with the main lines of Christian thought; one who pursues this sort of scholarship is quite unlikely to conclude, for example, that Jesus was really the second person of the divine Trinity who was crucified, died, and then literally rose from the dead the third day. As Van Harvey says, "So far as the biblical historian is concerned . . . there is scarcely a popularly held traditional belief about Jesus that is not regarded with considerable skepticism."[2]

I shall try to describe both of these kinds of scriptural scholarship. Then I'll ask the following question: how should a classical Christian, one who accepts "the great things of the gospel," respond to the deflationary aspect of HBC? How should she think about its apparently corrosive results with respect to traditional Christian belief? Given the extended Aquinas/Calvin model, I shall argue that she need not be much disturbed by the conflict between alleged results of HBC and Christian belief. That conflict does not offer a defeater for her acceptance of the great things of the gospel — nor, to the degree that those alleged results rest on epistemological assumptions she doesn't share, of anything else she accepts on the basis of biblical teaching.

Traditional Biblical Commentary

Christians typically accept the belief that the Bible is the Word of God and that in it the Lord intends to teach us important truths. (I don't for a moment mean to suggest that teaching truths is *all* that the Lord intends in Scripture: there is also raising affection, teaching us how to praise, how to pray, how to see the depth of our own sin, how marvelous the gift of salvation is, and a thousand other things.)

Of course, it isn't always easy to tell what the Lord *is* teaching us in a given passage. What he teaches is indeed true; still, sometimes it isn't clear just what he is teaching. Part of the problem is the fact that the Bible contains material of so many different sorts; it isn't in this respect at all

---

2. "New Testament Scholarship and Christian Belief," in *Jesus in History and Myth*, ed. R. Joseph Hoffman and Gerald A. Larue (Buffalo: Prometheus, 1986), p. 193.

like a contemporary book on theology or philosophy. It isn't a book full of declarative sentences, with proper analysis and logical development and all the accoutrements academics have come to know and love. The Bible does, indeed, contain sober assertion, but there is also exhortation, expression of praise, poetry, stories and parables, songs, devotional material, history, genealogies, lamentations, confession, prophecy, apocalyptic, and much else besides. Some of these (apocalyptic, for example) present real problems of interpretation (for us, at present): what exactly is the Lord teaching in Daniel, or Revelation? That's not easy to say.

Even if we stick to straightforward assertion, there are a thousand questions of interpretation. Just a couple of examples. In Matthew 5:17-20, Jesus declares that not a jot or a tittle of the law shall pass away and that "unless your righteousness surpasses that of the Pharisees and the teachers of the law, you will certainly not enter the kingdom of heaven"; but in Galatians Paul seems to say that observance of the law doesn't count for much. How can we put these together? How do we understand Colossians 1:24: "Now I rejoice in what was suffered for you, and I fill up in my flesh what is still lacking in regard to Christ's afflictions, for the sake of his body, which is the church"? Is Paul suggesting that Christ's sacrifice is incomplete, insufficient, that it requires additional suffering on the part of Paul or the rest of us? That seems unlikely. But then what does he mean? More generally, given that God is the principal author of Scripture, how shall we think about the apparent tensions Scripture displays? 1 John seems to say that Christians don't sin; in Paul's epistle to the Romans, he says that everyone sins; shall we draw the conclusion that there are no Christians? There are also problems about how to take the parables of Jesus. In Luke 18:1-8, for example, is Jesus suggesting that God will hear us just from sheer perseverance on our part, perhaps finally answering just because he's finally had enough? That doesn't sound right, but then how do we take the parable?

Scripture is inspired: what it teaches is true; yet it isn't always a trivial matter to tell what it *does* teach. Indeed, many of the sermons and homilies preached in a million churches every Sunday morning are devoted in part to bringing out what might otherwise be obscure in scriptural teaching. Given that the Bible is a communication from God to humankind, a divine revelation, there is much about it that requires deep and perceptive reflection, much that taxes our best scholarly and spiritual resources to the utmost. This fact wasn't lost on Augustine, Aquinas, Calvin, and the others I mentioned above; between them they wrote an impressively large number of volumes devoted to powerful reflection on the meaning and teachings of Scripture. (Calvin's commentaries alone run to more than twenty volumes.) Their aim was to determine as accurately as possible just what the Lord proposes to teach us in the Bible. Call this enterprise 'traditional biblical commentary' and note that it displays at least the following three features.

First, Scripture itself is taken to be a wholly authoritative and trustworthy guide to faith and morals; it is authoritative and trustworthy, because it is a revelation from God, a matter of God's speaking to us. Once it is clear, therefore, what the teaching of a given bit of Scripture is, the question of the truth and acceptability of that teaching is settled. In a commentary on Plato, we might decide that what Plato really meant to say was XYZ; we might then go on to consider and evaluate XYZ in various ways, asking whether it is true, or close to the truth, or true in principle, or superseded by things we have learned since Plato wrote; we might also ask whether Plato's grounds or arguments for XYZ are slight, or acceptable, or substantial, or compelling. These questions are out of place in the kind of scriptural scholarship under consideration. Once convinced that God *is* proposing XYZ for our belief, we do not go on to ask whether it is true, or whether God has made a good case for it. God is not required to make a case.

Second, an assumption of the enterprise is that the principal author of the Bible — the entire Bible — is God himself. Of course each of the books of the Bible has a human author or authors as well; still, the principal author is God. This impels us to treat the whole more like a unified communication than a miscellany of ancient books. Scripture isn't so much a library of independent books as itself a book with many subdivisions with a central theme: the message of the gospel. By virtue of this unity, furthermore (by virtue of the fact that there is just one principal author), it is possible to 'interpret Scripture with Scripture': if a given passage from one of Paul's epistles is puzzling, it is perfectly proper to try to come to clarity as to what God's teaching is in this passage by appealing not only to what Paul himself says elsewhere but also to what is taught elsewhere in Scripture (for example, the Gospel of John). Passages in the Psalms or Isaiah can be interpreted in terms of the fuller, more explicit disclosure in the New Testament; the serpent elevated on a pole to save the Israelites from disaster can be seen as a type of Christ (and thus as getting some of its significance by way of an implicit reference to Christ, whose being raised on the cross averted a greater disaster for the whole human race). A further consequence is that we can quite properly accept propositions that are inferred from premises coming from different parts of the Bible: once we see what God intends to teach in a given passage *A* and what he intends to teach in a given passage *B,* we can put the two together, and treat consequences of these propositions as themselves divine teaching.[3]

Third, and connected with the second point, the fact that the principal author of the Bible is God himself means that one can't always determine the meaning of a given passage by discovering what the human author had in mind. Of course various postmodern hermeneuticists aim to amuse by telling us that, in this case as in all others, the author's intentions have nothing whatever to do with the meaning of a passage, that the reader herself confers on the passage whatever meaning it has, or perhaps that even entertaining the idea of a text's having meaning is to fall into "hermeneutical innocence" — adding that such innocence is ineradicably sullied by its association with homophobic, sexist, racist, oppressive, and other unappetizing modes of thought. This is, indeed, amusing.

Returning to serious business, however, it is obvious (given that the principal author of the Bible is God) that the meaning of a biblical passage will be given by what it is that *the Lord* intends to teach in that passage, and it is precisely this that biblical commentary tries to discern. But we can't just assume that what the Lord intends to teach us is identical with what the human author had in mind; the latter may not so much as have thought of what is, in fact, the teaching of the passage in question. Thus, for example, Christians take the suffering servant passages in Isaiah to be references to Jesus; Jesus himself says (Luke 4:18-21) that the prophecy in Isaiah 61:1-2 is fulfilled in him; John (19:28-37) takes passages from Exodus, Numbers, Psalms, and Zechariah to be references to Jesus and the events of his life and death; Hebrews 10 takes passages from Psalms, Jeremiah, and Habakkuk to be references to Christ and events in his career, as does Paul for passages from Psalms and Isaiah in his speech in Acts 13. There is no reason to suppose the human authors of Exodus, Numbers, Psalms, Isaiah, Jeremiah, or Habakkuk had in mind Jesus' triumphal entry, his incarnation, or other events of Jesus' life and death — or, indeed, anything else explicitly about Jesus. But the fact that it is God who is the principal author here makes it quite possible that what we are to learn from the text in question is something rather different from what the human author proposed to teach.

---

3. Of course this procedure, like most others, can be and has been abused; that possibility in itself, however, is nothing against it, though it should serve as a salutary caution.

Historical Biblical Criticism

Traditional biblical commentary has been practiced from the beginning. As I mentioned above, however, the last couple of centuries have seen the rise of a very different kind of scriptural scholarship: historical biblical criticism (HBC). There is much to be grateful for with respect to HBC; it has enabled us to learn a great deal about the Bible that we otherwise might not have known. Furthermore, some of the methods it has developed (form criticism, source criticism, etc.) can be and have been employed to excellent effect in traditional biblical commentary.

HBC, however, differs importantly from traditional biblical commentary. HBC is fundamentally an Enlightenment project. It is an effort to look at and understand biblical books from a standpoint that relies on reason alone; that is, it is an effort to determine from the standpoint of reason alone what the scriptural teachings are and whether they are true. Thus HBC rejects the authority and guidance of tradition, creed, or any kind of ecclesial or 'external' epistemic authority. The idea is to see what can be established (or at least made plausible) using only the light of what we could call 'natural, empirical reason'. The faculties or sources of belief invoked, therefore, would be those that are employed in ordinary history: perception, testimony, and reason — but setting aside any proposition one knows by faith or by way of the authority of the church. Spinoza (1632-1677) already lays down the charter for this enterprise: "The rule for [biblical] interpretation should be nothing but the natural light of reason which is common to all — not any supernatural light nor any external authority."[4]

This project or enterprise is often thought of as part and parcel of the development of modern empirical science, and indeed practitioners of HBC like to wrap themselves in the mantle of modern science. The attraction is not just that HBC can perhaps share in the prestige of modern science, but also that it can share in the obvious epistemic power and excellence of the latter. It is common to think of science itself as our best shot at getting to know what the world is really like; HBC is, among other things, an attempt to apply these widely approved methods to the study of Scripture and the origins of Christianity. Thus Raymond Brown, a highly respected scriptural scholar, believes that HBC is "scientific biblical criticism";[5] it yields "fac-

---

4. *Tractatus Theologico-politicus*, 7.196.

5. *The Virginal Conception and Bodily Resurrection of Jesus* (New York: Paulist Press, 1973), p. 6.

tual results" (p. 9); he intends his own contributions to be "scientifically respectable" (p. 11); and he regards practitioners of HBC as investigating the Scriptures with "scientific exactitude" (pp. 18-19).[6]

What *is* it, exactly, to study the Bible scientifically? That's not so clear; there is more than one answer to this question. One theme that seems to command nearly universal assent, however, is that in working at this scientific project (however exactly it is to be understood) one doesn't invoke or employ any theological assumptions or presuppositions. You don't assume, for example, that the Bible is inspired by God in any special way, or contains anything like specifically divine discourse. You don't assume that Jesus is the divine Son of God, or that he rose from the dead, or that his suffering and death are in some way a propitiatory atonement for human sin.

You don't assume any of these things, they say, because, in pursuing science, you don't assume or employ any proposition which you know only by faith. (As a consequence, the meaning of a text will be what the human author intended to assert; divine intentions and teaching don't enter into the meaning.[7]) The idea, says E. P. Sanders, is to rely only on "evidence on which everyone can agree."[8] And according to Jon Levenson,

> Historical critics thus rightly insist that the tribunal before which interpretations are argued cannot be confessional or "dogmatic"; the arguments offered must be historically valid, able, that is, to compel the assent of *historians* whatever their religion or lack thereof, what-

6. See also John Meier, *A Marginal Jew: Rethinking the Historical Jesus* (New York: Doubleday, 1991), vol. 1, p. 1.

7. Thus Benjamin Jowett (the nineteenth-century master of Balliol College and eminent translator of Plato): "Scripture has one meaning — the meaning which it had to the mind of the prophet or evangelist who first uttered or wrote, to the hearers or readers who first received it" ("On the Interpretation of Scripture," in *The Interpretation of Scripture and Other Essays* [London: George Routledge, 1906], p. 36; quoted in Jon D. Levenson, *The Hebrew Bible, the Old Testament, and Historical Criticism* [Louisville: Westminster/John Knox Press, 1993], p. 78). Jowett was not a paragon of intellectual modesty, which may explain a poem composed and circulated by undergraduates at Balliol:

> First come I, my name is Jowett.
> There's no knowledge but I know it.
> I am the master of the college.
> What I don't know isn't knowledge.

8. *Jesus and Judaism* (Philadelphia: Fortress, 1985), p. 5.

ever their backgrounds, spiritual experiences, or personal beliefs and without privileging any claim of revelation.[9]

One very important caution: HBC is a *project* rather than a *method*. Someone who does traditional biblical commentary may use the same methods as someone who practices HBC; the difference comes out in what they assume or take for granted in carrying out their projects. In carrying out his work, one who does traditional biblical commentary assumes the main lines of Christian belief: the existence of God, the incarnation of the second person of the Trinity in Jesus, and so on. Those who practice HBC, on the other hand, propose to proceed without employing any theological assumptions or anything one knows by faith; these things are to be set aside. Instead, one proceeds scientifically, on the basis of reason alone. Beyond this, however, there is vastly less concord. What is to count as reason? Precisely what premises can be employed in an argument from reason alone? What exactly does it mean to proceed scientifically? Here HBC displays at least two distinct positions.

Troeltschian HBC

First, there is the sort of biblical criticism that draws on the thought and teaching of Ernst Troeltsch.[10] Troeltsch proposed several principles to be followed in scriptural interpretation, including the "principle of analogy": historical knowledge is possible because all events are similar in principle. This means that we must assume that the laws of nature in biblical times were the same as they are now. Within the HBC community, this principle is understood in such a way as to *preclude direct divine action in the world*. So in pursuing Troeltschian HBC, you have to assume that God has never acted directly in the world. Perhaps God created the world and perhaps he conserves it in being; but he does not and has not acted in the world

9. "The Hebrew Bible, the Old Testament, and Historical Criticism," in *Hebrew Bible*, p. 109. (An earlier version of this essay was published under the same title in *Hebrew Bible or Old Testament? Studying the Bible in Judaism and Christianity,* ed. John Collins and Roger Brooks [Notre Dame: University of Notre Dame Press, 1990].)

10. See especially his "Über historische und dogmatische Methode in der Theologie," in his *Gesammelte Schriften* (Tübingen: Mohr, 1913), vol. 2, pp. 729-53, and his article "Historiography," in James Hastings, *Encyclopedia of Religion and Ethics* (New York: Scribner's, 1967 [1909]).

beyond creation and conservation. So taken, this principle implies that God has not, in fact, specially inspired any human authors in such a way that what they write is really divine speech addressed to us; nor has he raised Jesus from the dead, turned water into wine, or performed miracles of any other sorts. Thus Rudolf Bultmann:

> The historical method includes the presupposition that history is a unity in the sense of a closed continuum of effects in which individual events are connected by the succession of cause and effect.

This continuum, furthermore, "cannot be rent by the interference of supernatural, transcendent powers."[11] So the idea here is that God perhaps created the world, but he never acts in it. And of course, this is in complete conflict with Christian belief.

Duhemian HBC

Troeltschian scriptural scholarship is one variety of HBC; there is also another and more moderate version, which we could call "Duhemian HBC." Pierre Duhem was a serious scientist. He was also a serious Catholic; and he was accused of allowing his religious and metaphysical views as a Christian to enter his physics in an improper way. Duhem resisted this suggestion, claiming that his Christianity didn't enter his physics in any way at all and *a fortiori* didn't enter it in an improper way.[12] Furthermore, the *correct* or *proper* way to pursue physical theory, he said, was the way in which he had in fact pursued it; physical theory should be completely independent of religious or metaphysical views or commitments.

Duhem's proposal, reduced to essentials, is that physicists shouldn't make essential use of religious or metaphysical assumptions in doing their physics. This proposal can obviously be applied far beyond the confines of physical theory: for example, to scriptural scholarship. Suppose we say that *Duhemian* scriptural scholarship is scriptural scholarship that doesn't

11. *Existence and Faith*, ed. Schubert Ogden (New York: Meridian Books, 1960), pp. 291-92. Note the suggestion that if God acted specially in the world he has created, he would be "interfering."

12. See the appendix to Duhem's *The Aim and Structure of Physical Theory*, trans. Philip P. Wiener, with a foreword by Prince Louis de Broglie (Princeton: Princeton University Press, 1954 [1906]). The appendix is entitled "Physics of a Believer."

involve any theological, religious, or metaphysical assumptions that aren't accepted by everyone in the relevant community. Thus the Duhemian scriptural scholar wouldn't take for granted either that God is the principal author of the Bible or that the main lines of the Christian story are in fact true; these are not accepted by all who are party to the discussion. She wouldn't take for granted that Jesus rose from the dead, or that any other miracle has occurred; she couldn't so much as take it for granted that miracles are possible (because their possibility is rejected by many who are party to the discussion). On the other hand, of course, Duhemian scriptural scholarship can't take it for granted that Christ did *not* rise from the dead or that *no* miracles have occurred, or that miracles are impossible.

Duhemian scriptural scholarship fits well with Sanders's suggestion that "what is needed is more secure evidence, evidence on which everyone can agree" (above, p. 98). It also fits well with John Meier's fantasy of "an unpapal conclave" of Jewish, Catholic, Protestant, and agnostic scholars, locked in the basement of the Harvard Divinity School library until they come to consensus on what historical methods can show about the life and mission of Jesus.[13] Among the proposed benefits of Duhemian HBC, obviously, are just the benefits Duhem cites: people of very different religious and theological beliefs can cooperate in this enterprise.

Conflict with Traditional Christianity

There has been a history of substantial tension between HBC and traditional Christians. Thus David Strauss in 1835: "Nay, if we would be candid with ourselves, that which was once sacred history for the Christian believer is, for the enlightened portion of our contemporaries, only fable."[14] Of course the unenlightened faithful were not so unenlightened that they failed to notice this feature of biblical criticism. Writing ten years after the publication of Strauss's book, William Pringle complains, "In Germany, Biblical criticism is almost a national pursuit. . . . Unhappily, [the critics] were but too frequently employed in maintaining the most dangerous errors, in opposing every inspired statement which the mind of man is un-

---

13. *Marginal Jew,* vol. 1, pp. 1-2.

14. *The Life of Jesus, Critically Examined,* trans. George Eliot (London: Chapman, 1846), p. 776. Originally published as *Das Leben Jesu kritisch bearbeitet* (Tübingen: Osiander, 1835).

able fully to comprehend, in divesting religion of its spiritual and heavenly character, and in undermining the whole fabric of revealed truth."[15] And Brevard Childs: "For many decades the usual way of initiating entering students in the Bible was slowly to dismantle the church's traditional teachings regarding scripture by applying the acids of criticism."[16]

HBC tends to discount miracle stories, taking it as axiomatic that miracles don't and didn't really happen or, at any rate, claiming that the proper method for HBC can't admit miracles as either evidence or conclusions. Perhaps Jesus effected cures of some psychosomatic disorders, but nothing that modern medical science can't explain. Many employing this method propose that Jesus never thought of himself as divine, or as the (or a) Messiah, or as capable of forgiving sin; thus Thomas Sheehan: "The crisis grows out of the fact now freely admitted by both Protestant and Catholic theologians and exegetes: that as far as can be discerned from the available historical data, Jesus of Nazareth did not think he was divine [and] did not assert any of the messianic claims that the New Testament attributes to him."[17]

Those who follow these methods are sometimes unusually creative; I can't resist mentioning some of the more innovative accounts. According to Barbara Thiering's *Jesus and the Riddle of the Dead Sea Scrolls*,[18] for example, Jesus was buried in a cave; he didn't actually die, and was revived by the magician Simon Magus, whereupon he married Mary Magdalene, settled down, fathered three children, was divorced, and finally died in Rome. G. A. Wells goes so far as to claim that our name 'Jesus', as it turns up in the Bible, is empty; like 'Santa Claus', it doesn't trace back to or denote anyone at all.[19] John Allegro apparently thinks there was no such person as Jesus of Nazareth; Christianity began as a hoax designed to fool the Romans and preserve the cult of a certain hallucinogenic mushroom

15. "Translator's Preface," *Calvin's Commentaries*, vol. 16, trans. William Pringle (Grand Rapids: Baker, 1979), p. vi. Pringle's preface is dated at Auchterarder, January 4, 1845.

16. *The New Testament as Canon: An Introduction* (Valley Forge, PA: Trinity Press International, 1994), p. xvii.

17. Thomas Sheehan, *The First Coming* (New York: Random House, 1986), p. 9. See my review, "Sheehan's Shenanigans: How Theology Becomes Tomfoolery," in *The Analytic Theist*, ed. James F. Sennett (Grand Rapids: Eerdmans, 1998).

18. San Francisco: HarperSanFrancisco, 1992.

19. "The Historicity of Jesus," in *Jesus in History and Myth*, ed. Hoffman and Larue, pp. 27ff. See also Richard Carrier's *On the Historicity of Jesus* (Sheffield, UK: Sheffield Phoenix Press, 2014).

(Amanita muscaria). Still, the name 'Christ' isn't empty: it is really a name of that mushroom.[20] As engaging a claim as any is that Jesus, while neither merely legendary nor actually a mushroom, was, in fact, an atheist, the first Christian atheist.[21] Of course these suggestions are not typical of HBC, and HBC is ordinarily much more sensible. Still, even if we set aside the lunatic fringe, Van Harvey is correct: "So far as the biblical historian is concerned . . . there is scarcely a popularly held traditional belief about Jesus that is not regarded with considerable skepticism."[22]

So HBC has not in general been sympathetic to traditional Christian belief; it has hardly been an encouragement to the faithful. The faithful, however, seem relatively unconcerned; they find traditional biblical commentary of great interest and importance, but the beliefs and attitudes of HBC have not seemed to filter down to them, in spite of its dominance in mainline seminaries. According to Van Harvey, "Despite decades of research, the average person tends to think of the life of Jesus in much the same terms as Christians did three centuries ago."[23] One possible reason is that there is no compelling or even reasonably decent argument for supposing that the procedures and assumptions of HBC are to be preferred, by Christians, to those of traditional biblical commentary. A little epistemological reflection enables us to see something further: the traditional Christian has good reason to reject the skeptical claims of HBC and continue to hold traditional Christian belief despite the allegedly corrosive acids of HBC.

We have both Troeltschian and Duhemian HBC. Consider the first. The Troeltschian scriptural scholar accepts Troeltsch's principles for historical research, under an interpretation according to which they rule out the occurrence of miracles and the divine inspiration of the Bible (along with the corollary that the Bible enjoys the sort of unity accruing to a book that has one principal author). It is not at all surprising, then, that the Troeltschian tends to come up with conclusions wildly at variance with those accepted by traditional Christians. Now if Troeltschian critics offered some good reasons to think that, in fact, these Troeltschian principles are *true,* then traditional Christians would have to pay attention; then they might be obliged to take the skeptical claims of historical critics seriously.

---

20. *The Sacred Mushroom and the Cross* (Garden City, NY: Doubleday, 1970).
21. Sheehan, *First Coming.*
22. See note 2, above.
23. "New Testament Scholarship," p. 194.

Troeltschians, however, apparently don't offer any such good reasons for those principles. So why should Christians pay much attention to claims that are based on them — based, that is, on the principle that God never acts specially in the world — with its implication that God did not raise Jesus from the dead and that the Bible is not in any special way inspired by God? If these claims depend essentially on those principles, Christians are entirely within their rights in ignoring these claims — at least until the Troeltschians come up with arguments for those principles.

What about Duhemian HBC? This is a very different kettle of fish. The Duhemian proposes to employ only assumptions that are accepted by everyone party to the project of biblical interpretation. She doesn't (for purposes of scholarship) accept the traditional Christian's views about the Bible or the life of Christ, but she doesn't accept Troeltsch's principles either. She doesn't assume that miracles did or could happen; but that is quite different from assuming that they didn't or couldn't, and she doesn't assume that either. She doesn't assume that the Bible is, in fact, divine revelation and hence authoritative and reliable; but she also doesn't assume that it isn't.

Of course that may not leave her a lot to go on. That is because there is enormous controversy with respect to scriptural scholarship; here the very foundations of the subject are deeply disputed. Does the Bible have one principal author, namely God himself? Is it divinely inspired, so that what it teaches is both true and to be accepted? The Bible reports miraculous happenings — the dead returning to life, a virgin birth, the changing of water into wine, healings of people blind or lame from birth: Are these to be taken more or less at face value, or dismissed as contrary to 'what we now know'? Is there an entry into the truth about these matters — faith or divine testimony by way of Scripture, for example — quite different from ordinary historical investigation?

These are all matters of ferocious dispute; but if we take no position on them, and proceed responsibly, what we come up with is likely to be pretty slender. A. E. Harvey, for example, proposes the following as beyond reasonable doubt from everyone's point of view (i.e., Duhemianly): "that Jesus was known in both Galilee and Jerusalem, that he was a teacher, that he carried out cures of various illnesses, particularly demon-possession and that these were widely regarded as miraculous; that he was involved in controversy with fellow Jews over questions of the law of Moses: and that he was crucified in the governorship of Pontius Pilate."[24]

24. *Jesus and the Constraints of History* (Philadelphia: Westminster Press, 1982), p. 6.

Or consider John Meier's monumental *A Marginal Jew: Rethinking the Historical Jesus.* (The first volume has 484 pages; the second has 1,055 pages; there is also a third and a fourth volume.) Meier aims to be Duhemian: "My method follows a simple rule: it prescinds from what Christian faith or later Church teaching says about Jesus, without either affirming or denying such claims" (p. 1). (I think he also means to eschew assumptions incompatible with traditional Christian belief.) Meier's fantasy of "an unpapal conclave" of Jewish, Catholic, Protestant, and agnostic scholars, locked in the basement of the Harvard Divinity School library until they come to consensus on what historical methods can show about the life and mission of Jesus, is thoroughly Duhemian. This conclave, he says, would yield "a rough draft of what that will-o'-the-wisp 'all reasonable people' could say about the historical Jesus" (p. 2).

Meier sets out, judiciously, objectively, carefully, to establish that consensus. What is striking about his conclusions, however, is how meager they are, and how tentative. About all that emerges from Meier's painstaking work is that Jesus was a prophet, a proclaimer of an eschatological message from God, someone who performed powerful deeds, signs, and wonders that announce God's kingdom and also ratify his message. As a Duhemian, of course, Meier can't add that these signs and miracles involve special or direct divine action; nor can he say that they don't. He can't say that Jesus rose from the dead, or that he did not; we can't conclude that Scripture is specially inspired, or that it isn't.

Duhemian HBC, therefore, limits itself to what is accepted by all participants. The traditional Christian, on the other hand, takes the Bible to be divine testimony; she will therefore believe that, for example, Jesus rose from the dead, even if that proposition is not accepted by the "unpapal conclave." But then she needn't be fazed by the fact that Duhemian HBC doesn't support her views about what Jesus did and said. It need not present her with an intellectual or spiritual crisis. An analogy: we can imagine a renegade group of whimsical physicists proposing to reconstruct physics by refusing to use any beliefs that comes from *memory,* say, or perhaps memory of anything more than one minute ago. Perhaps something could be done along these lines, but it would be a poor, paltry, truncated, trifling thing. And now suppose that, say, Newton's laws or special relativity turned out to be dubious and unconfirmed from this point of view: that would presumably give little pause to more traditional physicists. This truncated physics could hardly call into question physics of the fuller variety.

Similarly here. The traditional Christian thinks he knows *by faith* that Jesus was divine and that he rose from the dead. Hence, he will be unmoved by the fact that these truths are not especially probable on the evidence to which Duhemian HBC limits itself — that is, evidence which explicitly excludes what one knows by faith. Why should that matter to him? For a Christian to confine himself to the results of Duhemian HBC would be a little like trying to mow your lawn with a nail scissors or paint your house with a toothbrush; it might be an interesting experiment if you have time on your hands, but otherwise why limit yourself in this way?

More generally, then: HBC is either Troeltschian or Duhemian. If the former, then it begins from assumptions entailing that much of what the traditional Christian believes is false; it comes as no surprise, then, that its conclusions are at odds with traditional belief. But it is also of little direct concern to the classical Christian. It offers her no reason at all for rejecting or modifying her beliefs; it also offers little promise of enabling her to achieve better or deeper insight into what actually happened. As for Duhemian HBC, this variety of historical criticism omits a great deal of what she sees as relevant evidence and relevant considerations. It is therefore left with little to go on. Again, the fact that it fails to support traditional belief need not be upsetting to the believer; given those limitations, that is only to be expected, and it casts no doubt at all on Christian belief. Either way, therefore, the traditional Christian can rest easy with the claims of HBC; she need feel no obligation, intellectual or otherwise, to modify her belief in the light of its claims and alleged results.

CHAPTER NINE

Defeaters? Pluralism

Historical biblical criticism, as I argued, doesn't or at least doesn't automatically present Christian believers with a defeater. But what about the facts of religious pluralism, the fact that the world displays a bewildering and kaleidoscopic variety of religious and antireligious ways of thinking, all pursued by people of great intelligence and seriousness? There are theistic religions, but also at least some nontheistic religions (or perhaps nontheistic strands of religion) among the enormous variety of religions going under the names 'Hinduism' and 'Buddhism'. Among the theistic religions, there are Christianity, Islam, Judaism, strands of Hinduism and Buddhism, American Indian religions, some African religions, and still others. All of these differ significantly from each other. Moreover, some individuals — despite this panoply of religious options — reject all religions.

Given that I know of this enormous diversity, isn't it somehow arbitrary, or irrational, or unjustified, or unwarranted (or maybe even oppressive and imperialistic) to endorse one of them as opposed to all the others? How can it be right to select and accept just one system of religious belief from all this blooming, buzzing confusion? Won't that be in some way irrational? And doesn't this pluralism therefore present a defeater for Christian belief? As the sixteenth-century writer Jean Bodin put it, "each is refuted by all."[1] According to John Hick: "In the light of our accumulated knowledge of the other great world faiths, [Christian

---

1. *Colloquium Heptaplorneres de rerum sublimium arcanis abditis,* written by 1593 but first published in 1857. English trans. Marion Kuntz (Princeton: Princeton University Press, 1975), p. 256.

exclusivism] has become unacceptable to all except a minority of dog-matic diehards."[2]

This is the problem of pluralism, and our question is whether a knowledge of the facts of pluralism constitutes a defeater for Christian belief. The specific problem I mean to discuss can be thought of as follows. To put it in an internal and personal way, I find myself with religious beliefs, and religious beliefs that I realize aren't shared by nearly everyone else. For example, I believe both

> (1) The world was created by God, an almighty, all-knowing, and per-fectly good personal being (i.e., the sort of being who holds beliefs, has aims and intentions, and can act to accomplish these aims)

and

> (2) Human beings require salvation, and God has provided a unique way of salvation through the incarnation, life, sacrificial death, and resurrection of his divine Son.

Now I realize there are many who do not believe these things. First, there are those who agree with me on (1) but not (2): there are non-Christian theistic religions. Second, there are those who don't accept either (1) or (2), but nonetheless do believe that there is something beyond the natural world, a something such that human well-being and salvation depend on standing in a right relation to it. And third, in the West and since the Enlightenment, anyway, there are people — *naturalists,* we may call them — who don't believe any of these three things.

One way to react to these other religious responses to the world is to continue to believe what I have all along believed; I learn about this diversity, but continue to believe (i.e., take to be true) such propositions as (1) and (2) above, consequently taking to be false any beliefs, religious or otherwise, that are incompatible with (1) and (2). Following current practice, I shall call this *exclusivism;* the exclusivist holds that the tenets or some of the tenets of *one* religion — Christianity, let's say — are in fact true; he adds, naturally enough, that any propositions, including other religious beliefs, that are incompatible with those tenets are false. Our question, therefore, is whether it is possible to be a *rational* exclusivist;

---

2. *God Has Many Names* (Philadelphia: Westminster, 1982), p. 27.

our question, that is, is whether I have a defeater for my Christian belief in my knowledge of the facts of religious pluralism. Must I recognize that the existence of these other ways of thinking gives me a defeater for my own?

Perhaps the most important suggestion in the neighborhood is that there is something *arbitrary* about accepting Christian belief. This arbitrariness is thought to have both a moral and an intellectual component. The *moral* charge is that there is a sort of egoism, perhaps pride or *hubris,* in accepting beliefs when one realizes both that others do not accept them and that in all likelihood one possesses no arguments that would convince those dissenters. The *epistemic* charge also focuses on arbitrariness: here the claim is that the exclusivist is treating similar things differently, thus falling into intellectual arbitrariness. And the idea would be that in either case, when the believer comes to see these things, then she has a defeater for her belief, a reason for giving it up or, at the least, holding it with less firmness. I shall focus on the moral charge, dealing with the charge of epistemic arbitrariness along the way. And here we shall have to broaden the notion of a defeater. We've been thinking all along about *epistemic* defeaters, where, roughly speaking, I get an epistemic defeater for a belief *B* that I hold when I acquire a new belief *B** such that it would be irrational to continue to believe *B* as long as I believe *B**. But there are also *moral* defeaters. I get a moral defeater for a belief *B* I hold when I acquire a new belief *B** such that it would be immoral for me to continue to believe *B* as long as I believe *B**.

It is the moral kind of defeater that is at issue here. The moral charge is that there is a sort of self-serving arbitrariness, an arrogance or egoism, in accepting such propositions as (1) or (2); one who accepts them is guilty of some serious moral fault or flaw. According to Wilfred Cantwell Smith (as we saw in Chapter Two), "except at the cost of insensitivity or delinquency, it is morally not possible actually to go out into the world and say to devout, intelligent, fellow human beings: '. . .we believe that we know God and we are right; you believe that you know God, and you are totally wrong.'"[3] So what can the believer say for herself?

It must be conceded immediately that if she believes (1) or (2), then she must also think that those who believe something incompatible with them are mistaken and believe what is false; that's just logic. Furthermore, she must also believe that those who do not believe as she does — those who believe neither (1) nor (2), whether or not they believe their negations

3. *Religious Diversity* (New York: Harper & Row, 1976), p. 14.

— fail to believe something that is true, deep, and important. Of course she *does* believe this deep and important truth; hence she must see herself as *privileged* with respect to those others. There is something of great value, she must think, that *she* has and *they* lack. They are ignorant of something — something of great importance — of which she has knowledge.

But does this make her properly subject to the above censure? Am I really arrogant and egoistic just by virtue of believing something I know others don't believe, where I can't show them that I am right? I can't see how. Of course I must concede that there are a variety of ways in which I can be and have been intellectually arrogant and egoistic; I have certainly fallen into this vice in the past, will no doubt fall into it in the future, and am not free of it now. Still, suppose I think the matter over, consider the objections as carefully as I can, realize that I am finite and furthermore a sinner, certainly no better than those with whom I disagree, and indeed inferior both morally and intellectually to many who do not believe what I do. But suppose it *still* seems clear to me that the proposition in question is true: am I really immoral in continuing to believe it? The eighteenth-century Quakers believed slavery was wrong. They realized, of course, that most of their contemporaries did not share that belief, and they also realized that they had no arguments that would convince their contemporaries. Given that they were thus out of step with the majority, they no doubt reflected carefully on this belief. If, on reflection, slavery still seemed to them wrong, seriously wrong, could they really be doing something immoral in continuing to believe that slavery was wrong? I don't think so. In the same way, if, after careful reflection and thought, you find yourself convinced of (1) and (2), how could you properly be taxed with egoism for believing them? Even if you knew others did not agree with you? So I can't see how the moral charge against exclusivism can be sustained, and if it can't, this charge does not provide a moral defeater for Christian belief.

Consider King David. He saw the beautiful Bathsheba bathing, was smitten, sent for her, slept with her, and made her pregnant. After the failure of various stratagems to get her husband, Uriah, to think *he* was the father of the baby, David arranged for Uriah to be killed by telling his commander to "put Uriah in the front line where the fighting is fiercest. Then withdraw from him so he will be struck down and die" (2 Sam. 11:15). Then the prophet Nathan came to David and told him a story about a rich man and a poor man. The rich man had many flocks and herds; the poor man had only a single ewe lamb, which grew up with his children. The rich man had unexpected guests. Instead of slaughtering one of his own sheep, he took the poor man's single ewe lamb, slaughtered it, and served it to his guests. David exploded in anger: "The man who did this deserves to die!" Then, in one of the most riveting passages in all the Bible, Nathan turns to David, stretches out his arm, points to him, and thunders, *"You are that man!"* And then David sees what he has done.

My interest here is in David's reaction to the story. I agree with David: such injustice is utterly and despicably wrong. I believe that such an action is wrong, and I believe that the proposition that it *isn't* wrong — either because really *nothing* is wrong, or because even if *some* things are wrong, *this* isn't — is false. As a matter of fact, there isn't a lot I believe more strongly. I recognize, however, that plenty of people disagree with me; many believe that some actions are *better*, in one way or another, than others, but that none is really right or wrong in the full-blooded sense in which I think *this* action is.

Once more, I doubt that I could find an argument to show them that I am correct and they incorrect. Furthermore, their beliefs might seem the same to them from the inside, so to speak, as my beliefs seem to me. Am I then being arbitrary, treating similar cases differently in continuing to hold, as I do, that in fact that kind of behavior *is* dreadfully wrong? I don't think so. Am I wrong in thinking racial bigotry despicable and dead wrong, even though I know that others disagree, and even though I know I have no arguments that would convince them? Again, I don't think so.

And the reason here is this: in each of these cases, the believer in question doesn't really think the beliefs in question *are* on a relevant epistemic par. She may agree that she and those who dissent are equally convinced of the truth of their belief. Still, she must think that there is an important epistemic difference: she thinks that somehow the other person has made a mistake, or has a blind spot, or hasn't been wholly attentive, or hasn't received some grace she has, or is blinded by ambition or pride or mother love or something else; she must think that she has access to a source of warranted belief the other lacks. If the believer concedes that she *doesn't* have any special source of knowledge or true belief with respect to Christian belief — no *sensus divinitatis*, no internal instigation of the Holy Spirit, no teaching by a church inspired and protected from error by the Holy Spirit, nothing not available to those who disagree with her — *then*, perhaps, she can properly be charged with an arbitrary egoism, and *then*, perhaps, she will have a defeater for her Christian belief. But why should she concede these things? She will ordinarily think (or at least *should* ordinarily think) that there are indeed sources of warranted belief that issue in these beliefs. (And here we have a way in which the epistemologist can be of use to the believer.)

She believes, for example, that in Christ, God was reconciling the world to himself; she may believe this on the basis of what the Bible or church teaches. She knows that others don't believe this and furthermore that they don't accept the Bible's (or church's) authority on this or any other point. She has an explanation: there is the testimony of the Holy Spirit (or of the divinely founded and guided church); the testimony of the Holy Spirit enables us to accept what the Scriptures teach. It is the Holy Spirit who seals it upon our hearts, so that we may certainly know that God speaks; it is the work of the Spirit to convince our hearts that what our ears receive has come from him.

She therefore thinks she is in a better epistemic position with respect to this proposition than those who do not share her convictions; for she believes she has the witness of the divinely guided church, or the internal testimony of the Holy Spirit, or perhaps still another source for this knowledge. She may be *mistaken,* in so thinking, deluded, in serious and debilitating error, but she needn't be *culpable* in holding this belief. That is because she nonculpably believes that she has a source of knowledge or true belief denied those who disagree with her. This protects her from epistemic egoism and arbitrariness.

But wouldn't that very thought — that she has a source of knowledge or true belief denied those who disagree with her — be itself an instance of epistemic egoism? How could you think a thing like that without displaying epistemic egoism? Well, it happens all the time. A biology teacher gives a test: one of the students gives an answer the teacher disagrees with; the teacher quite properly believes that he is in a better epistemic position, by virtue of years of training and study. He is not egoistic in so thinking. The serious believer, therefore, need not be either intellectually arrogant or arbitrary if she can reasonably think that she is not on an epistemic par with those who disagree with her. Can she sensibly think that? She can, if she can sensibly think that the extended Aquinas/Calvin model presented above is in fact correct.

But don't the realities of religious pluralism count for *anything?* Is there nothing at all to the claims of the pluralists?[4] Could that really be right? Of course not. For at least some Christian believers, an awareness

---

4. See W. P. Alston, "Religious Diversity and Perceptual Knowledge of God," *Faith and Philosophy* 5, no. 4 (October 1988): 433ff.

of the enormous variety of human religious responses *does* seem to reduce the level of confidence in their own Christian belief. It doesn't or needn't do so by way of an *argument*. Indeed, there aren't any respectable arguments from the proposition that many apparently devout people around the world dissent from (1) and (2) to the conclusion that (1) and (2) are false or can be accepted only at the cost of moral or epistemic deficiency.

Nevertheless, knowledge of others who think differently can reduce one's degree of belief in Christian teaching. From a Christian perspective, this situation of religious pluralism is itself a manifestation of our miserable human condition; and it may indeed deprive a Christian of some of the comfort and peace the Lord has promised his followers. It can also deprive the believer of the *knowledge* that (1) and (2) are true, even if they *are* true and he *believes* that they are. Since degree of warrant depends in part on degree of belief, it is possible, though not necessary, that knowledge of the facts of religious pluralism should reduce his degree of belief and hence the degree of warrant (1) and (2) enjoy for him; it can therefore deprive him of knowledge of (1) and (2). He might be such that if he *hadn't* known the facts of pluralism, then he would have known (1) and (2), but now that he *does* know those facts, he doesn't know (1) and (2). In this way he may come to know less by knowing more.

Things *could* go this way. On the other hand, they *needn't* go this way. Consider once more the moral parallel. Perhaps you have always believed it deeply wrong for a counselor to use his position of trust to seduce a client. Perhaps you discover that others disagree; they think it more like a minor peccadillo, like running a red light when there's no traffic. You think the matter over more fully, imaginatively re-create and rehearse such situations, become more aware of just what is involved in such a situation (the breach of trust, the injustice and unfairness, the nasty irony of a situation in which someone comes to a counselor seeking help but receives only hurt), and come to believe even more firmly that such an action is wrong. In this way, this belief could acquire more warrant for you by virtue of your learning and reflecting on the fact that some people do not see the matter your way.

Something similar can happen in the case of religious beliefs. A fresh or heightened awareness of the facts of religious pluralism could bring about a reappraisal of one's religious life, a reawakening, a new or renewed and deepened grasp and apprehension of (1) and (2). From the perspective of the extended A/C model, it could serve as an occasion for a renewed and more powerful working of the belief-producing processes by which we come to apprehend (1) and (2). In this way knowledge of the facts of pluralism could initially serve as a defeater; in the long run, however, it can have precisely the opposite effect. The facts of religious pluralism, therefore, like historical biblical criticism, do need not constitute a defeater for Christian belief.

CHAPTER TEN

Defeaters? Evil

I turn finally to the most formidable candidate for a defeater for theistic belief: the traditional 'problem of evil'. Our world contains an appalling amount and variety both of suffering and of evil. I'm thinking of *suffering* as encompassing any kind of pain or discomfort: pain or discomfort that results from disease or injury, or oppression, or overwork, or old age, but also disappointment with oneself or with one's lot in life (or that of people close to one), the pain of loneliness, isolation, betrayal, unrequited love; and there is also suffering that results from awareness of others' suffering. I'm thinking of *evil*, fundamentally, as a matter of free creatures' (human or otherwise) doing what is wrong, including particularly the way we human beings mistreat and savage each other. Often pain and suffering result from evil, as in some of the events for which the twentieth century will be remembered — the Holocaust, the horrifying seventy-year-long Marxist experiment in eastern Europe with its millions of victims, the villainy of Pol Pot and his followers, the waves of genocide in Bosnia and Africa. Of course much suffering and evil is banal and everyday, and is none the better for that.

Now the evil and suffering in our world has, indeed, baffled believers in God. This bafflement and perplexity are widely represented in Christian and Hebrew Scriptures, especially, though by no means exclusively, in the Psalms and the book of Job. Faced with the shocking concreteness of a particularly horrifying example of suffering or evil in his own life or the life of someone close to him, a believer can find himself tempted to take toward God an attitude he himself deplores — an attitude of mistrust, or suspicion, or bitterness, or rebellion. Such a problem, broadly speaking, is a spiritual or pastoral problem. A person in its grip may not be much tempted to doubt the existence or even the goodness of God; nevertheless he may resent God, fail to trust him, be wary of him, be unable to think of him as a loving Father, think of him as if he were far off and unconcerned.

A Powerful Atheological Argument from Evil?

Many, however, have argued that knowledge of the amount, variety, and distribution of suffering and evil ('the facts of evil') confronts the believer with a problem of quite another sort. These facts, they argue, can serve as the premise of a powerful argument against the very existence of God — against the existence, that is, of an all-powerful, all-knowing, and wholly good person who has created the world and loves the creatures he has created. Such arguments go all the way back to the ancient world, to Epicurus (341-270 B.C.), whose reasoning is repeated in the eighteenth century by that arch-skeptic philosopher, David Hume (1711-1776):

> Epicurus' old questions are yet unanswered.
> Is he willing to prevent evil, but not able? then he is impotent.
> Is he able, but not willing? then he is malevolent.
> Is he both able and willing? whence then is evil?[1]

And the claim is that knowledge of this argument constitutes a defeater for theistic belief (belief in God) — and if for theistic belief, then, of course, also for Christian belief.

Our question, therefore, is whether knowledge of the facts of evil *does* constitute a defeater for theistic and Christian belief. Does this knowledge make it the case that I cannot continue to hold Christian belief *rationally?* Note that this is not the traditional problem of theodicy: I will not be making any attempt to "justify the ways of God to man" or to give an answer to the question why God permits evil generally or why he permits some specially heinous forms of evil.[2] Our question is, instead, *epistemological:* given that theistic and Christian belief can have warrant in the ways I

---

1. *Dialogues Concerning Natural Religion,* ed. Richard Popkin (Indianapolis: Hackett, 1980), p. 63. Hume puts the argument in the mouth of Philo, widely thought to represent Hume's own views.

2. For a suggestion along those lines, see my "Supralapsarianism, or 'O Felix Culpa,'" in *Christian Faith and the Problem of Evil,* ed. P. van Inwagen (Grand Rapids: Eerdmans, 2004).

have suggested, does knowledge of the facts of evil provide a defeater for this belief? Does it threaten to make such belief irrational or unwarranted?

Of course, the answer need not be the same for all Christians: perhaps the facts of suffering and evil, in our sad world, do not constitute such a defeater for very young Christians, or for culturally insulated Christians, or for Christians who know little about the suffering and evil our world contains, or for those who don't have an adequate appreciation of the seriousness of what they do know about. Our question, however, is about "intellectually sophisticated adults in our culture" (above, p. 89); can I be mature, both intellectually and spiritually, be aware of the enormous and impressive amounts and depths of suffering and evil in our world, be aware also of the best anti-theistic arguments starting from the facts of evil, and still be such that Christian belief is rational and warranted for me? Could it still have warrant sufficient for knowledge, for me? I shall argue that the right response is, "Yes indeed." And it isn't that this can be so just for an exceptional few. I shall argue that for any serious Christian with a little epistemology, the facts of evil, appalling as they are, offer no obstacle to warranted Christian belief.

Now until thirty or thirty-five years ago, the favored sort of argument from evil was for the conclusion that there is *logical inconsistency* in what Christians believe. They believe both that there is such a person as God (a person who is omnipotent, omniscient, and wholly good), and also that there is evil in the world; it isn't logically possible (so went the claim) that both of these beliefs be true. The claim was that the existence of God is *logically incompatible* with the existence of evil; since the theist is committed to both, theistic belief is clearly irrational.

At present, however, it is widely conceded that there is nothing like straightforward contradiction or necessary falsehood in the joint affirmation of God and evil; the existence of evil is not logically incompatible (even in the broadly logical sense) with the existence of an all-powerful, all-knowing, and perfectly good God.[3]

Of course that doesn't necessarily suffice to get the theist off the hook. There is also no logical contradiction in the thought that the earth is flat, or that it rests on the back of a turtle, which rests on the back of

---

3. The essential point is that it is possible, in the broadly logical sense, that (1) it was not within God's power to create free persons who always do only what is right, and (2) the value of having free creatures outweighs the disvalue of the evil they do. For a development of the argument, see my *God, Freedom, and Evil* (Grand Rapids: Eerdmans, 1978), pp. 7ff.

another turtle, and so on, so that it's turtles all the way down; nevertheless these views (given what we now think we know) are irrational. (You would be distressed if your grown children adopted them.) Those who offer arguments from evil have accordingly turned from the claim that the existence of God is flatly incompatible with that of evil to *evidential* or *probabilistic* arguments of one sort or another.

Here the claim is not that Christian belief is logically inconsistent, but rather that the facts of evil offer *powerful evidence against* the existence of God. These evidential arguments are also typically probabilistic: in the simplest cases, they claim that the existence of God is unlikely or improbable with respect to the facts of evil. So the typical atheological claim at present is not that the existence of God is *incompatible* with that of evil; it is rather that evil presents a strong evidential or probabilistic case against the existence of God.

Well, suppose evil does constitute evidence, of some kind, against theism: what follows from that? Not much. There are many propositions I believe that are true and rationally accepted, and such that there is evidence against them. The fact that Peter is only three months old is evidence against his weighing nineteen pounds; nevertheless I might rationally (and truly) believe that's how much he weighs. Is the idea, instead, that the existence of God is improbable with respect to our *total evidence,* all the rest of what we know or believe? To show this, the atheologian would have to look into all the evidence *for* the existence of God — the traditional ontological, cosmological, and teleological arguments, as well as many others;[4] he would be obliged to weigh the relative merits of all of these arguments, and weigh them against the evidential argument from evil in order to reach the indicated conclusion. This would not be easy.

Still further, suppose theism *were* improbable with respect to the rest of what I believe; alternatively, suppose the rest of what I believe offered evidence *against* theism and none *for* it. What would follow from that? Again, not much. There are many true beliefs I hold (and hold in complete rationality) such that they are unlikely given the rest of what I believe. I am playing poker; it is improbable on the rest of what I know or believe that I have just drawn to an inside straight; it doesn't follow that there is even the slightest irrationality in my belief that I have just filled an inside straight.

---

4. See my "Two Dozen (or So) Theistic Arguments," available as an Appendix to Deane-Peter Baker, ed., *Alvin Plantinga: Contemporary Philosophy in Focus* (Cambridge: Cambridge University Press, 2007), pp. 203ff.

The reason, of course, is that this belief doesn't depend, for its warrant, on its being appropriately probable on the rest of what I believe; it has a quite different source of warrant, namely, perception. Similarly for theism: everything really turns, here, on the question whether, as I have been arguing, theism has or may have some source of warrant — perception of God, or the *sensus divinitatis*, or faith and the internal instigation of the Holy Spirit — distinct from its probability with respect to the other propositions I believe.

The Strongest Case from Evil

There is no cogent argument for the conclusion that the existence of evil is incompatible with the existence of God; there is also no serious evidential or probabilistic argument from evil; fair enough. Still, suffering and evil do constitute *some* kind of problem for at least *some* believers in God; the Old Testament is full of examples. Indeed there is the agonized cry uttered by Jesus Christ himself: "My God, my God, why have you forsaken me?" — a cry in which he is echoing the words of Psalm 22. The book of Job is a searching and powerful exploration of the facts of evil and human responses to them. Job is incensed; he thinks God is unfair to him and challenges God to explain and justify himself. Countless others, in the grip of their own cruel suffering or the suffering of someone close to them, have found themselves angry with God; as a result of suffering and evil in one's life, one can become resentful of God, mistrusting him, antagonistic and hostile to him.

Still, these situations don't typically produce a defeater for theistic belief. It isn't as if Jesus, or the Psalmist, or Job is at all inclined to give up theistic belief. The problem is of a different order; it is a spiritual or pastoral problem rather than a defeater for theistic belief. Perhaps God permits my father, or my daughter, or my friend, or me to suffer in the most appalling way. I may then find myself thinking as follows: "No doubt he has all those dandy divine qualities and no doubt he has a fine reason for permitting this abomination — after all, I am no match for him with respect to coming up with reasons, reasons that are utterly beyond me — but what he permits is appalling, and I hate it!" I may want to tell him off face to face: "You may be wonderful, and magnificent, and omniscient and omnipotent (and even wholly good) and all that exalted stuff, but I utterly detest what you are doing!" A problem of this kind is not really an evidential problem at all, and it isn't a defeater for theism.

But perhaps that's not the only realistic reaction here: perhaps I *could* react in this way, but aren't there other rational reactions? Might I not just give up belief in a good God altogether? Couldn't suffering and evil, under some circumstances, at any rate, actually serve as a defeater for belief in such a God? The list of atrocities human beings commit against others is horrifying and hideous; it is also so long, so repetitious, that it is finally wearying. Occasionally, though, new depths are reached:

> A young Muslim mother in Bosnia was repeatedly raped in front of her husband and father, with her baby screaming on the floor beside her. When her tormentors seemed finally tired of her, she begged permission to nurse the child. In response, one of the rapists swiftly decapitated the baby and threw the head in the mother's lap.[5]

Such things are absolutely horrifying; it is painful even to consider them, to bring them squarely before the mind. To introduce them into cool philosophical discussion like this is distressing and can seem callous. And now the question: Wouldn't a rational person think, in the face of this kind of appalling evil, that there just couldn't be an omnipotent, omniscient, and wholly good person superintending our world? Perhaps she can't give a demonstration that no perfect person could permit these things; perhaps there isn't a good probabilistic or evidential anti-theistic argument either: but so what? Isn't it just apparent, just evident that a being living up to God's reputation couldn't permit things like that? Don't I have a defeater here, even if there is no good argument from evil?

Something like this, I think, is the best version of the anti-theistic case from evil. The claim is essentially that one who is properly sensitive and properly aware of the sheer horror of the evil displayed in our somber and unhappy world will simply see that no being of the sort God is alleged to be could possibly permit it. This is a sort of inverse *sensus divinitatis*: perhaps there is no good argument from evil; but no argument is needed. An appeal of this sort will proceed, not by rehearsing arguments, but by putting the interlocutor in the sort of situation in which the full horror of the world's suffering and evil stands out clearly in all its loathsomeness. Indeed, from the atheological point of view, giving an argument is counterproductive here: it permits the believer in God to turn his attention

---

5. Eleonore Stump, "The Mirror of Evil," in *God and the Philosophers,* ed. Thomas Morris (New York: Oxford University Press, 1994), p. 239.

away, to avert his eyes from the abomination of suffering, to take refuge in antiseptic discussions of possible worlds, probability functions, and other arcana. It diverts attention from the situations that in fact constitute a defeater for belief in God.

No Defeater for Someone Who Is Fully Rational

Suppose we look into this claim — the claim that a clear look at evil provides a defeater for belief in God. Recall first that a defeater for a belief *depends on the rest of what I believe;* whether my new belief is a defeater for an old belief depends upon what else I believe and what my experience is like. I believe that tree is a maple; you tell me it's really an elm. This will defeat my belief that it's a maple if I think you know what you are talking about and aim to tell the truth, but not if I think you are even less arboreally informed than I, or that there is only a fifty-fifty chance that you are telling what you take to be the truth. Coming to see the full horror of the evil the world displays might be a defeater for theistic belief for *some* but not for *others.*

What I want to argue first is that if classical Christianity is true, then the perception of evil is not a defeater for belief in God for someone who is *fully rational,* someone whose cognitive faculties are functioning properly. From the point of view of classical Christianity (at any rate according to the A/C model), this includes also the proper function of the *sensus divinitatis.* Someone in whom this process was functioning properly would have an intimate, detailed, vivid, and explicit knowledge of God; she would have an intense awareness of his presence, glory, goodness, power, perfection, wonderful attractiveness, and sweetness; and she would be as convinced of God's existence as of her own.

She might therefore be *perplexed* by the existence of this evil in God's world — for God, she knows, hates evil with a holy and burning passion — but the idea that perhaps there just *isn't* any such person as God would no doubt not so much as cross her mind. Confronted with evil and suffering, such a person might ask herself why God permits it; the facts of evil may be a spur to inquiry as well as to action. If she finds no answer, she will no doubt conclude that God has a reason that is beyond her ken; she won't be in the least inclined to doubt that there *is* such a person as God. For someone fully rational, on the A/C model, the existence of evil doesn't so much as begin to constitute a defeater for belief in God.

How about Other Believers?

On the A/C model, therefore, the facts of evil do not constitute any sort of defeater for theistic belief for a fully *rational* person. Nevertheless (so the wily atheologian will claim), that fact is at best of dubious relevance with respect to the question whether Christian believers in God — the ones there actually are — have a defeater for theism in the world's ills. For according to Christian doctrine itself, none of us human beings enjoys that pristine condition of complete rationality. The *sensus divinitatis* has been heavily damaged by sin; for most of us most of the time the presence of God is not evident. For many of us (much of the time, anyway) both God's existence and his goodness are a bit shadowy and evanescent, nowhere nearly as evident as the existence of other people or the trees in the backyard. For a fully rational person, knowledge of the facts of evil may constitute no defeater for theism; for actual fallen human beings, however (so the claim goes), they do.

To pursue this line, however, would be to neglect still another feature of Christian belief: that the damage to the *sensus divinitatis* is in principle and increasingly repaired in the process of faith and regeneration. The person of faith may be once more such that, at least on some occasions, the presence of God is completely evident to her. In addition, she knows of the divine love revealed in the incarnation, the unthinkable splendor of the whole Christian story, the suffering and death of Jesus Christ, himself the divine and unique Son of God, on our behalf. Of course this knowledge does not provide an answer to the question, Why does God permit evil? It is nonetheless of crucial importance here.

I read of one more massive atrocity and am perhaps shaken. But then I think of the inconceivably great love displayed in Christ's suffering and death, his willingness to empty himself and take on the nature of a servant, his willingness to suffer and die so that we sinful human beings can achieve redemption; and my faith may be restored. I still can't imagine why God permits this suffering, or why he permits people to torture and kill each other, or why he permits gigantic and horrifying social experiments such as Nazism and communism; nevertheless I see that he is willing to share in our suffering, to undergo enormous suffering himself, and to undergo it for our sakes. Confronted with a particularly loathsome example of evil, therefore, I may find myself inclined to question God, perhaps even to be angry and resentful: "Why should I or my family suffer to promote his (no doubt exalted) ends, when I don't have even a glimmer of an idea as to how my suffering contributes to some good?" But then I think of the divine willingness to endure greater suffering on my behalf and am comforted or, at any rate, quieted.

Note that probabilities have little to do with the matter. Such a person doesn't reason thus: it's not very likely that an omnipotent, omniscient, and wholly good person would permit such atrocities — but it's more likely that such a being who was himself willing to undergo suffering on our behalf would permit them. The comfort involved here doesn't go by way of probabilistic reasoning.

There is another important consideration. It is plausible to think that the best possible worlds God could have actualized contain the unthinkably great good of divine incarnation and redemption — but then, of course, also sin and suffering. God chooses one of these worlds to be actual; and in it, humankind suffers. Still, in this world there is also the marvelous opportunity for redemption and for eternal fellowship with God, an inconceivably great good that vastly outweighs the suffering we are called upon to endure.[6] Still further, in being offered eternal fellowship with God, we human beings are invited to join the charmed circle of the Trinity itself; and perhaps that invitation can be issued only to creatures who have fallen, suffered, and been redeemed. If so, the condition of humankind is vastly better than it would have been, had there been no sin and no suffering. *O felix culpa,* indeed!

Accordingly, those who have faith (those in whom the process of regeneration is taking place) will also be such, according to the model, that the presence and goodness of God is to some degree evident to them; so for them the belief that there is such a person as God will have considerable warrant. They too, then, like someone in whom the *sensus divinitatis* had never been damaged, will feel little or no inclination to atheism or agnosticism when confronted with cases of horrifying evil. They may be perplexed; they may be shocked; they may be spurred both to action and to inquiry by the presence of appalling evil in God's world; but ceasing to believe will not be an option. If the salient suffering is their own, they may concur with the author of Psalm 119:75-76: "I know, O Lord, that your laws are righteous, and in faithfulness you have afflicted me. May your unfailing love be my comfort, according to your promise to your servant."

The fact is they may even enjoy a blessed contentment. Here is a

---

6. Paul continues in Rom. 8:18: "I consider that our present sufferings are not worth comparing with the glory that will be revealed in us."

letter from Guido de Bres (author of the Belgic Confession, 1561) to his wife, written shortly before he was hanged:

> Your grief and anguish, troubling me in the midst of my joy and glad-ness, are the cause of my writing you this present letter. I most ear-nestly pray you not to be grieved beyond measure. . . .
>
> I am shut up in the strongest and wretchedest of dungeons, so dark and gloomy that it goes by the name of the Black Hole. I can get but little air, and that of the foulest. I have on my hands and feet heavy irons which are a constant torture, galling the flesh even to my poor bones. But, notwithstanding all, my God fails not to make good His promise, and to comfort my heart, and to give me a most blessed content.[7]

De Bres suffered greatly; yet he enjoyed "a most blessed content." The furthest thing from his mind, no doubt, was the thought that maybe there wasn't any such person as God, that maybe he had been deceived all along. And this continuing to believe betrays no irrationality at all: it isn't as if he had a defeater for theistic belief in his suffering, but some-how suppressed it and (perhaps by way of wishful thinking) continued to believe anyway. No, his belief was instead a result of the proper function of the cognitive processes — a rejuvenated *sensus divinitatis,* the internal instigation of the Holy Spirit — that produce belief in God.

Aren't There Any Defeating Circumstances for Theistic Belief?

Of course, most of us are not in the spiritual condition of Guido de Bres. Not nearly all of us enjoy that comfort and content in the face of suffering. As Calvin points out (*Institutes,* III.ii.15), most of us sometimes have dif-ficulty thinking that God is, indeed, benevolent toward us; and even the great masters of the spiritual life sometimes find themselves in spiritual darkness. Christians must concede that their epistemic and spiritual situ-ations differ widely from person to person, and within a given person from time to time. Aren't there any conditions at all, then, in which the facts of evil constitute a defeater for Christian or theistic belief?

---

7. Quoted in Cornelius Plantinga Jr., *A Place to Stand* (Grand Rapids: Board of Pub-lications of the Christian Reformed Church, 1981), p. 35.

I should think the right answer is "Probably not." Consider a person in whom the *sensus divinitatis* doesn't work at all well, a person who believes in God in a thoughtless and superficial way, a person for whom the belief has no real vivacity or depth or liveliness — perhaps such a person, on coming to a deep appreciation of the facts of evil, will give up theistic belief. However, that doesn't show that this person has a defeater for theistic belief. She has such a defeater only if, in those circumstances, it would be irrational, contrary to proper cognitive function, to continue to believe in God. She has such a defeater only if it is part of our cognitive design plan to give up theistic belief in those circumstances. But we have no reason to think that our design plan mandates giving up theistic belief in those circumstances. The design plan includes the proper function of the *sensus divinitatis;* how things actually go when that process does not function properly *could* be part of the design plan; more likely, though, it is an unintended by-product rather than a part of the design plan.

Nevertheless, let's suppose, just for purposes of argument, that as a matter of fact such a person really *does* have a defeater for theistic belief. What it is important to see, here, is that if she does have a defeater, it is only because of a failure of rationality somewhere in her noetic structure (perhaps there is dysfunction with respect to the *sensus divinitatis*). And now suppose we return to our original question: does a person S who believes that there is such a person as God have a defeater in the facts of evil? We can now see that there is no reason to think so. The very fact that S continues in theistic belief is evidence that the *sensus divinitatis* is functioning properly to at least some degree in her. It is perhaps *possible* (if failure to believe in these circumstances *is* part of the design plan) that she has a defeater; but there is no reason to think so. I conclude, therefore, that in all likelihood believers in God do not have defeaters for theistic belief in knowledge of the facts of evil.

By way of conclusion then: I can't, of course, claim to show that there are no defeaters for Christian or theistic belief. But I can (and do) claim that three of the most plausible candidates for that post — historical biblical criticism, pluralism, and suffering and evil — do not in fact succeed.

Afterword

In this book I argued first (in Chapter One) that there really is such a thing as Christian belief and that we can, in fact, talk and think about God. In

Chapter Two I distinguished *de jure* from *de facto* objections to Christian belief; the former are to the effect that such belief is intellectually or rationally questionable, even if true. Although *de jure* objections have been very common ever since the Enlightenment, it isn't easy to tell just what the objections are supposed to be. I argued that no viable *de jure* objection lies in the neighborhood of justification, conceived in terms of duty and obligation. I proposed next to argue that there are no plausible *de jure* objections that are independent of *de facto* objections. The only initially promising candidate for such a *de jure* objection to Christian belief, I said, can be approached by way of Freud's claim that Christian belief does not have *warrant,* or at any rate warrant sufficient for knowledge. Freud, however, simply presupposes that theistic and hence Christian belief is false; therefore this alleged *de jure* objection fails to be independent of the *truth* of Christian belief. I argued further that the same fate will befall any alleged *de jure* objection formulated in terms of warrant.

In Chapter Three, I presented the Aquinas/Calvin model of how it is that belief in God can have warrant, and even warrant sufficient for knowledge. In Chapters Four, Five, and Six, I extended the A/C model in such a way as to deal both with sin and with the full panoply of Christian belief: Trinity, incarnation, atonement, resurrection. Chapter Seven dealt with a couple of objections to this model. Finally, in Chapters Eight through Ten, I considered contemporary historical biblical criticism, pluralism, and the age-old problem of evil as actual or potential defeaters for Christian belief. None of these, I argued, presents a serious challenge to the warrant Christian belief can enjoy if the model, and indeed Christian belief, is, in fact, true.

But *is* it true? This is the really important question. And here we pass beyond the competence of philosophy. In my opinion no argument with premises accepted by everyone or nearly everyone is strong enough to support full-blown Christian belief, even if such belief is, as I think it is, more probable than not with respect to premises of that kind. Speaking for myself and not in the name of philosophy, I can say only that it does, indeed, seem to me to be true, and to be the maximally important truth.

Index